
ADOPTED TEENS
ONLY

Published book reviews by Danea Gorbett can be found at
www.parentsreview.org

Parent in Control by Gregory Bodenhamer

Too Old For This, Too Young For That by Unger Mosatche

*Grounded for Life?! Stop Blowing Your Fuse and Start Communicating
with Your Teenager* by Louise Felton Tracy

6 Steps to an Emotionally Intelligent Teenager by James Windell

ADOPTED TEENS ONLY

A Survival Guide to Adolescence

Danea Gorbett

iUniverse Star
New York Lincoln Shanghai

ADOPTED TEENS ONLY
A Survival Guide to Adolescence

Copyright © 2004, 2007 by Danea Gorbett

All rights reserved. No part of this book may be used or reproduced by any means, graphic, electronic, or mechanical, including photocopying, recording, taping or by any information storage retrieval system without the written permission of the publisher except in the case of brief quotations embodied in critical articles and reviews.

iUniverse Star
an iUniverse, Inc. imprint

iUniverse books may be ordered through booksellers or by contacting:

iUniverse
2021 Pine Lake Road, Suite 100
Lincoln, NE 68512
www.iuniverse.com
1-800-Authors (1-800-288-4677)

Because of the dynamic nature of the Internet, any Web addresses or links contained in this book may have changed since publication and may no longer be valid.

The views expressed in this work are solely those of the author and do not necessarily reflect the views of the publisher, and the publisher hereby disclaims any responsibility for them.

ISBN: 978-1-58348-481-4 (pbk)
ISBN: 978-0-595-89169-6 (ebk)

Printed in the United States of America

To my husband, Rich,
who stood by me through the writing process.

To my children, Richard and Abigail,
who provided the encouragement to keep writing.

To my parents, Patti and Dan,
who gave me the experiences to share.

Contents

Acknowledgments

Thank-you to the many adoptees, adoptive parents, and birth parents who shared their personal stories with me. A very special thank-you to Kathy Austin, Connie and Dan Craig, DeAnne Harbison, Therese Maring, Patty Nemec, Denise and Mark Orlando, and Amy Sears for all of the ideas and suggestions you provided.

Preface

My story begins like so many other stories told to adoptees. My mother was a young teenager when she found out she was pregnant. She was in a relationship with my biological father but he too was young and had no money to raise a child. The decision had basically been made to place me for adoption. That was the plan until my mother decided at the last minute to keep me at home with her parents, my grandparents. My father's family would not allow him to have any contact with me or my mom's family at all. Unfortunately, her life didn't happen the way she planned. She got married when I was two but not to my father. My step-father and his family adopted me as one of their own.

This type of family is pretty normal today, but about the time you were born it was an unusual family arrangement. Despite the complex relationships underneath our family, we were a fairly normal family. I had a dad who worked and a mom who stayed at home. I had two sets of grandparents that treated me the same. I was pretty lucky.

The whole time I was growing up I would often wonder why this happened to me and how different my life could have been if my two biological parents had gotten married or if I had been placed for adoption. The older I got, the more I understood how life worked. The more I understood, the angrier I became at my biological father.

Also, the older I got, the more differences I noticed between me and my family. I didn't feel like I belonged to either my mom's family or my "adopted" dad's family. It seemed I just didn't fit in anywhere. I didn't look like anybody in my family. I certainly didn't share the same interests or talents. Sometimes I felt all alone. I blamed my biological father for these feelings as well. The anger was really starting to grow then.

Adolescence brought about new challenges. My mother got divorced right before I hit the teen years. This was just about the time I really started becoming curious about my biological father. I spent a lot of time wondering if I had brothers or sisters, if I looked like him and if I was more like him than I was like the family I had grown up knowing.

Finally, I got the courage up to ask my mom about my biological father. At that time, I just wanted to know the basic facts about his life, maybe see some current pictures and to know what type of job he had and if he went to college. Next thing I knew I was meeting my biological grandfather.

Nobody ever asked me if I wanted to meet my biological father's family. Everybody else thought it would help me adjust to being a teenager if I could connect with my biological father's side of the family. I was not mature enough to stand up for myself, so the meeting with my biological grandfather happened as scheduled.

The meeting was okay. I got my questions answered, saw some pictures and then considered it a closed case at the age of thirteen. The rest of the family thought it would be a great idea if I met my biological father. I thought, "Sure, maybe when I'm twenty-one." The following week I was on my way to meeting the rest of my biological relatives that I had never met, my father included.

Everything was happening so fast. This whole process became very disturbing to me when I found out no one but his parents knew I existed. Although, I imagine my biological father's family was just as disturbed to find out he had a teenage daughter. I just couldn't understand how I could have been kept a secret for so long. The fact that I had been kept a secret for so long combined with my anger really set the stage for my future relationship with my new family.

During this process nobody stopped to ask what I was thinking, feeling or what I wanted. Everyone else determined the course of my teenage years. An arrangement was set up where I would spend the weekend with my biological father and his family every third weekend. The only thing I wanted to do was go to the movies with my friends and hang out at their houses on the weekends. The anger and resentment continued to grow. In fact, this process was so traumatic for me that I actually blocked most of it out and still do not remember many of the details.

Eventually I went to college and severed the relationship between me and my father. I resolved to never have contact with my father or his family ever again. Even though I was still very angry about this part of my life, I decided not to let it interfere with the rest of my life.

I lived for quite a few years very happy and mostly fulfilled. I got a college degree in psychology in hopes of helping troubled teenagers. I worked in a group home for teenagers whose parents had either lost custody of them or their parents could not handle them at home. Eventually I started working on a master's degree in special education to continue my interest in helping teenagers. Although, a little void in my life existed that never quite got filled up, but it only bothered me occasionally during major life events like when I got married, had kids, and when my maternal grandmother died.

One day my life came to a halt when I received a letter from my father. I was not prepared to have contact of any sort from him, but somehow I had a feeling I was not getting out of this one. During the next two weeks I spent a great deal of time wondering how I should answer his letter. Do I take this opportunity to say all the things I wanted to say since I was a young child or do I keep pretending my anger was not bothering me. Finally, I decided he needed to hear my side of the story and how his decision affected my life.

Writing that letter and mailing it was therapeutic. My anger was released and I finally stood up for myself. I told him a relationship could not happen unless I had all of my questions answered truthfully. I thought that chapter in my life was over and I could get back to my normal routine. I did for a short while.

Then one day my phone rang. The caller ID came up "unknown." I had never answered unknown calls before, but for some strange reason that day I answered the phone. It was my father telling me he had the answers to my questions. Once again, I was completely shocked that this could be happening. I agreed to meet in person. The meeting would take place after the holidays, in a month.

As far as I was concerned, the relationship was still over even if he was able to provide me with all of the answers to my questions. Needless to say, our meeting was not warm and fuzzy. My father asked me if I would consider starting over in a new relationship. I agreed to think about it, but I had no intention of complicating my life unnecessarily.

However, several of my friends, who happened to be adopted, convinced me to rethink my decision. They would have given anything to be in my position. I decided to give it a shot. Once I agreed to get to know my father, my life went into a tailspin. My mind regressed back to my teenage years where I temporarily left my issues. I started doing some research and talking to people to make sense out of what was happening to me.

I was amazed to learn my experiences were similar to what adopted teenagers in open adoptions experience today. When I realized how similar our situations were, I knew I had to share my knowledge and expertise with the adopted teenagers of today. I started collecting stories from adoptees, birth parents, and adoptive parents. In fact, you will find many of these stories in italics throughout this book. However, the names and certain identifying details have been changed to protect the privacy of the individuals and their families.

As you read this book, keep in mind every section is based on true stories. The stories are backed up with extensive research. All of the individuals who contributed their stories hope you find the answers to the questions you may have that come out of being an adopted teenager.

Introduction

Has anyone ever discussed with you the unique aspects of being an adopted teenager? Do you know what thoughts adopted teens typically have over the course of adolescence about being adopted? Have you ever wondered why your parents act the way they do? Do you want to know what sorts of experiences your birth mother felt in placing you for adoption or how she feels today? Have you ever thought about searching for your birth parents and what you might find when you do?

This book will help you work through the questions you are concerned about right now as a teenager. As you read the quotes from adoptees you will realize what you are feeling is typical. Chapter One, "Am I Normal?," explains common thoughts and feelings that teen adoptees have throughout adolescence. You will be asked challenge questions at the end of each section to help you pinpoint just exactly where your feelings are coming from and how they might be affecting you. Solutions are offered to help you move past these specific challenges. You will also find suggestions for making a plan to overcome your challenges.

Chapter Two, "Adoptive Parents," provides information about what your parents are going through having an adopted teenager in the house. You will be surprised to learn they are dealing with a lot of the same issues you are right now. Their concerns are coming to the surface at the same time as yours. This always makes for an interesting time in both of your lives.

Chapter Three focuses mostly on birth mothers since birth mothers are generally very willing to talk about their experiences. Most birth-mother stories are tear-jerkers so do not expect happy endings in this chapter. Even though birth fathers are not addressed in this chapter, this does not mean they are not affected by adoption. Quite the opposite is true. Many birth fathers feel strong emotions about placing their baby for adoption.

You will find information about searching for your birth parents in Chapter Four. Even if you do not plan on searching for your birth parents, you should still take time to check out some of the issues related to searching. When people ask why you are not searching for your birth parents you can list off several good reasons. If you do plan on searching, you will be armed with the necessary tools to survive the searching process.

The search process is brought to a full circle in Chapter Five with reunions. If you would like to reunite with a birth parent, this chapter will let you know what to expect and how to prepare for the meeting. Reuniting with your birth parent can bring many surprises.

Chapter Six discusses the problems you might encounter when bringing up the possibility of getting information about your birth parents from your parents. You will get some practical suggestions from parents of teenagers on how to bring up sensitive topics. Parents of all personality types contributed information, so you are sure to find tips that will work with your parents.

The topics and discussions in this book may leave you feeling emotionally charged, so do not skip the last chapter, Looking Forward, where you will learn about all the positives of being adopted. At times you may think all of this turmoil will never end, but it will and you will be a much better person for having gone through these experiences.

Before we get started though, you will want to put your adoption experiences into perspective so you can see why your views are different from the views of other teen adoptees. Let's get started.

Did you know you are a part of a large social experiment? You are the first generation of teenagers to come out of open adoptions. If you had been born just a few years earlier, you would have been whisked away from your birth mother as soon as you were born. Your parents would have been chosen to pick you up at the hospital only because they were next on the list. No personal information would have been shared between your birth mother and adoptive parents. They would have never even met. The records would have been sealed for life.

In your case, your birth parents likely had the option to choose the family they believed would give you the best chances for success. Your birth parents probably interviewed several potential adoptive families before making their final decision. They poured over family income records, educational backgrounds, personal beliefs, and parenting practices before settling on the adoptive parents you know today.

That may seem like a lot of work, but that was the easiest part of your adoption. Now your birth parents and your adoptive parents had to agree on the adoption arrangements. They had to come to terms with just how open the adoption would be for them and you. Their decision on the level of openness back then still continues to affect you today.

Your birth parents may have believed it was in your best interest if they did not interfere with your adoptive parents' job of providing a stable home for you. At the other end of the spectrum, your birth parents might have been part of your life since birth. Most adoptions lie somewhere in between these two extremes. Maybe a file is kept active so your adoptive parents can let your birth parents know what you are doing, what your interests are, and what you look like. Your parents may provide pictures and home movies for your birth parents. On the other hand, your birth parents may send pictures and letters to you. These letters might be given to you when you reach a certain age, generally eighteen. Your file might have been kept open for as little as a few months after your birth or it may be kept active today.

Given the different levels of openness in the adoption process, you will feel things differently than other adoptees your age. Adoption issues are specific to the individual. No two family situations are the same. Every feeling is normal, because there is no wrong or right way to feel. What you feel will depend on your family experiences, personality, peer relationships, and your perceptions of all your experiences combined.

The degree of openness will definitely shape your feelings and experiences on your journey to adulthood. If you are part of a truly open adoption, you will experience stress in particular areas of your life, unlike your counterparts in closed adoptions. You may feel pressure to choose your "favorite" set of parents. You have to decide where to spend birthdays, holidays, and vacations. Your birth parents and adoptive parents have to coordinate schedules for visits. In some ways, the issues you deal with are similar to a divorced family. You are juggling two sets of parents. However, you do not struggle with identity issues near as much as teens in closed adoptions. Nor do you fantasize about your birth parents or feel rejection or abandonment.

If you are part of a more closed adoption, you will have different stressors. You may be struggling with forming an identity. You have to deal with issues of loss, anger, and rejection. However, you do not have to make tough decisions about how to divide your time between your family members. You probably have a more traditional family lifestyle.

Your individual personality combined with the decisions made by both sets of your parents will affect how you experience adolescence as an adoptee. Your life will be viewed from a different perspective than your peers who have been raised by their biological parents.

As you progress through puberty you will notice physical changes along with mental changes. Your childhood definitions of family will change during adolescence. You will begin to ask yourself many new questions about your adoptive family, your birth parents, and how adoption has affected your life. Sometimes these questions lead to more questions. Some questions get answered and some may never get answered. People in nonadopted families have questions about their families that never get answered either. This is just a fact of life.

Learning to live with these questions while trying to become your own independent person can be quite challenging. Not knowing your biological family can make adolescence more complex while you are trying to figure out how and where you fit in with your friends, family, and the world around you.

You are entering a stage in your life where your main goal is to try out different roles to see which ones are most comfortable for you. You will be trying to tie your past, your present, and your future together to form a complete picture of yourself. You might find this period of your life frustrating if you do not have knowledge about your biological parents.

Unless your parents are adopted, they will not be able to fully understand what you are feeling. Your parents have not lived the same experiences you have lived. However, these caring people can provide the support you will need while sorting out the issues you are facing. Basically your parents may hold the key to getting the answers to your questions.

Most importantly when you start asking questions and seeking answers about your biological roots, you are doing the same thing that your peers do. It is perfectly normal to want to know where you came from and how you got to where you are today. Searching for genetic connections is a natural part of being human. As for your peers, they just ask their parents outright or look at their family members for the answers. You cannot look around for answers. The natural result is curiosity of the unknown.

Chapter One

Am I Normal?

Fantasizing and Curiosity. Do you find yourself fantasizing about your birth parents from time to time? Do you ever wonder if other adopted teens are as curious about their biological beginnings as you are? According to one study 41 percent of adopted teens admitted to thinking about their adoption from monthly to daily (Benson et. al. 1997). The following list of questions about birth parents is common among adopted teenagers:

- What do my birth parents look like?
- What talents do my birth parents have?
- Do I look anything like my birth parents?
- Do I have any siblings?
- Did my birth parents love each other?
- Did my birth parents marry each other?
- Did my birth mother hold me and feed me after I was born?
- Where do my birth parents live?
- What are the living conditions of my birth parents?
- What traditions and customs do my birth parents practice?
- What religion are my birth parents?

I want to know if there is someone out there who looks just like me. I want to know if I have a sibling that looks like me. I want to know if I look like my biological parents. I want to know if I have any sisters.

Most people do not have to ask these questions. Most people have grown up hearing stories about their aunts, uncles, and grandparents. Most people know what their biological family members look like. Most people know what talents tend to run in their family.

You cannot look around for the answers to your questions. You have not been raised hearing stories about how your grandparents struggled during the Great Depression. You do not know which men in your family fought in World War II. Photographs of your biological grandparents, aunts, and uncles do not exist. You do not know how long your birth mother was in labor. There are no stories of your birth mother's ride to the hospital. You have no pictures of your biological parents holding you in the hospital. Pictures of you in the hospital may not exist at all.

The missing pieces of information about your birth parents and biological relatives will be more important to you now than when you were younger. You will become curious as to how being adopted has made you who you are today. You will also start to notice differences between you and your parents. You may notice big differences between you and your siblings, especially if your siblings were not adopted. You will naturally try to close the gaps by creating images in your mind to fit your story.

In other words, you will be daydreaming about your birth parents. Daydreaming is your mind's way of filling in the blanks. You may even create elaborate plans in which your birth parents come find you. You may imagine what life would be like to live with them. You may even fantasize they are famous or exceptionally wealthy. Maybe you see them as poor, on public aid or in drug abuse clinics. Adopted teens often believe their birth parents were wild teenagers having sex all the time. The scenarios are endless.

When I was younger I would fantasize that my birth parents were poor. I would think that I would find them, especially my mother, and my mom would adopt them too.

Other types of daydreams involve people around you in everyday situations. You have probably heard stories about lost relatives finding each other in strange places so you know it is possible. When you walk down the street do you look for people who might be related to you? For example, let's say you were waiting for a friend to meet you outside of your favorite hangout. While you were waiting you noticed a lady walking out of the building. You also noticed you looked just like her. You shared the same hair color, eye color, facial features, and body type. She seemed the right age to be your birth mother. You even know your birth mother lives in the same town as you. Could she have been your birth mother?

> *When I pulled open the door of the building to go inside, a man was coming out. I immediately recalled the face of my birth father from the pictures. The resemblances were remarkable. I still swear to this day it was him. Whenever I visited that city from that point on, I would constantly be looking for him.*

These thoughts are not only perfectly normal, but they can be helpful for you in dealing with your curiosity and your desire to connect with relatives. They allow you to construct some logical view of your birth family. Your mental picture of your birth parents may be totally wrong or perfectly right. Your daydreams fill in missing pieces of your story that you are trying to put together.

> *When things with my family weren't going so well, I imagined my father finding me and rescuing me from all my problems. In my dream everything turned out great. I used to have this daydream a lot.*

If you have some information about your birth parents, you may try to fill in the missing pieces by acting in ways you imagine your birth parents would act. This is a way of establishing a biological connection to your birth parents. Remember, this information might be true or it might be false. For example, if your parents told you your birth mother had a reputation for being a rebel, you may find yourself seeking out friends that fit that stereotype. You may think it is okay to stay out past curfew because it is in your genes. You feel closer to your birth mother by acting this way.

> *I sometimes wonder if I was a little wilder than I would have been. I don't know if I was wild because I had three older and wilder brothers or because I was always told my biological mother had me and was not married.*

Another situation that can occur is if you put together a portrait of your birth parents based on true information at the time of your birth. However, your biological parents have grown up since you were born. New attitudes and behaviors developed with age. The picture in your mind of your birth parents based on old information does not mean they continued down the same path throughout their life. If you do not have current information, you cannot know for certain what they are like today.

> *I was always told my birth father and his parents refused to support my mother even though they acknowledged I was his child. I grew up thinking he was irresponsible and probably a jerk. I rationalized in my mind it was probably for the best that I didn't grow up knowing him. Some years later I did get to know him and realized my vision of him was totally wrong. In fact, after he graduated from school he went to college to work in a career saving people's lives. I can't believe I spent my time growing up thinking I came from such a bad person.*

If your parents have given you no information about your birth parents or they refuse to discuss them with you, you may think they are really bad people. You may assume there must be something really terrible about them. Again, this can lead you to dreaming up some pretty awful images of your birth parents that may or may not be true.

Daydreaming is normal behavior, but the important point to remember is they are just fantasies. Try not to get too caught up in them. Fantasy can be a healthy way of sorting out your feelings and trying to make sense of yourself. On the other hand, making decisions about how to live your life by what you think your biological parents are like would be betraying your own true self.

Challenge. What happens in your daydreams? Who are you talking to? What are you doing? How do your dreams end? Are you happy? Have you been saved from something or someone? Are you avoiding something or someone? Do you feel you are constantly obsessing about these dramas playing in your mind? Are these daydreams interfering with your ability to concentrate in school, at home or with your peers?

Solution. Chances are someone in your family has some of the answers to your questions. While you were being adopted, your parents surely confided in someone. Most likely it will be your parents who will provide this information, but your aunts, uncles, and grandparents are all good sources to talk to if you cannot ask your parents. Also, you may need the help of a social worker or attorney. In which case, you will have to ask your parents for financial help and emotional support to get the answers to your questions.

Plan. Decide who you are going to talk to about your birth parents, what you are going to ask them, and when you are planning on asking them? Put a deadline on your plan so you won't be tempted to procrastinate!

Being Different. Like other teenagers, you just want to fit in with everyone else. You probably spend hours upon hours finding the right outfit to wear, listening to the most popular music, watching the most recent movies, and figuring out how to buy the latest gadgets. Your main goal is to be like your peers. Being one of the crowd is very important for you.

Being an adopted teen sometimes makes you more sensitive to comments that point out how you are not like your peers. Comments that did not used to bother you in elementary school may start making you really mad. Feelings of being different can come from not only you but from your friends, teachers, and family.

> *People who knew my situation would call me names and would joke around about me being adopted. It always hurt my feelings, but I became really sensitive to it when I was a teenager. It made me feel different than the rest of my friends when I wanted to be just like them.*

Class projects can remind you of differences in your family as well. If you have ever had to make a family tree with pictures, you know how those types of projects make you feel. The differences become apparent when all of the pictures and information is laid out in front of you.

> *One day in class my teacher gave us an assignment in which we had to write a paper about a family member we were like and how they served as our role model. The worst part was we had to share it with the class. I was so different from my family that I couldn't think of a single person I was similar to. I was amazed at how quickly all of the kids around me could think of someone. I knew I couldn't get out of this assignment so I ended up creating a fictitious relative so no one would notice and ask me questions.*

The differences between you and your parents may have taken on an added significance to you, too. You start to question why your parents like to stay home when you are always on the go. On the other hand, they may not understand why you are so rowdy when they prefer to be quiet. If you have siblings that are biologically related to your parents, the differences may become even more apparent. You may feel the differences are a frequent reminder that you are the adopted one. For instance, if your siblings and parents all have brown hair and you have blond hair, you cannot help but notice this. These differences may or may not bother you too much, but you will still feel the differences.

When I was a kid I used to go swimming. I would get so black when I was young. She [a relative] was watching me because my parents were out of town. I was probably five or six. When your skin gets all together it's really black. She thought it was dirt on my knees. She was scrubbing my knees. I said, "Don't you understand that's my skin." Why don't they understand?

Extended family members may treat you differently than your siblings or cousins. In fact, you may have cousins that take great pride in pointing out that you are not a "real" member of the family. Maybe you receive cheaper gifts than your cousins. Maybe your grandparents go to your cousins' sporting events but not yours. Older members of your family can be quite obvious in their remarks about you being adopted. Some extended family members may not accept you at all as part of their family. This may be especially true if you are a transracial adoptee. On the bright side, you are probably developing a very positive quality—tolerance.

Even your parents may be pointing out the racial differences between you and them. Your well-meaning parents are trying to immerse you in your native culture. They have spent a great deal of time creating extensive collections of articles from your birth country and ancestral heritage. They have also spent a great deal of time with you exploring places that emphasize your cultural traditions. However, it seems the more they try to make you feel part of a group, the more they are making you feel you are different.

On the other hand, you may enjoy standing out from the rest of your peers and family members. You welcome comments from others about being adopted. Someone asking you personal questions does not bother you in the least bit. In fact, the more attention you receive from your friends and family, the better. This is perfectly normal, too.

If comments from others bother you, it is best to politely bring up how these comments and actions make you feel. Many times the person does not even realize they are hurting your feelings. However, you will have others who just do not care. In which case, you can ignore them when possible or try to create some humor out of the situation.

Once again, there is no right or wrong way to feel. Everybody is different from one another. Even identical twins have different personalities, interests, and abilities. Learning to appreciate yourself for who you are as a person will help you reach your goals in life.

> **Challenge.** How do you feel different; your skin color, your ethnicity, your hair, your eyes, your personality, your interests, your talents, the fact you are adopted? Do you have two moms and one dad or two dads and one mom? How are you different from your parents, your peers and the people in your community? Do these differences interfere with how you interact with your peers and family?

> **Solution.** This is tricky, because you cannot change many of the things that make you feel different. Do not despair. You can always change your perception. Instead of focusing on the ways you are different from everyone else, think about the ways you are the same as everyone else. Changing your perception may take quite a bit of practice. You have been thinking the same thoughts for years. Keep practicing and your thoughts will change.

> **Plan.** Make a list of the similarities you share with your friends and family. Include favorites such as weekend hangouts, movies, music, cars, vacation spots, style of clothes, sports, hobbies, clubs, restaurants, television shows, and social views. Don't forget to include all of the things you don't like, too. You will be surprised at just how alike you are to your friends and parents! Every time you start to feel different, remind yourself of the similarities.

Genetic History. Wanting to know your genetic history is very normal. You may want to know if it is possible that you will reach six feet tall. If you are struggling with a weight issue, it would be comforting to know that weight problems tend to be hereditary within your biological family. Perhaps that bit of knowledge could help you in your struggle to overcome a weight issue. If you are a girl and wondering when puberty will start, you could predict it based on your birth mother's history.

> *As a teenager I used to have these bags under my eyes. I tried everything to get rid of them and nothing worked. I was very self-conscious about my eyes. I felt like people were always staring at them. I even wanted to have plastic surgery to have them removed. As soon as I met my birth father I knew where my eyes came from. He had the exact same bags under his eyes. After that I knew there was no reason to keep trying to fight genetics. I just didn't worry about it anymore.*

Despite advances in medicine, family background information can be helpful in predicting the outcome of your own health. Many diseases and mental health conditions are genetically passed along bloodlines. If you know your background, then you know what to watch for as you grow older. You also know what to avoid, which increases your chances of having a healthy body.

> *I feel that it is the utmost importance that adoptees have their medical and genetic history available to them. With all the genetic disorders that are known today, I feel that each adoptee should have all information available. I also feel that this information should not be from the time of the adoption. The information should be current.*

> *What if I have a genetic disease that could have been prevented if I had early detection knowing that I was at a high risk?*

In fact, one of the main reasons adoptees search is to obtain a medical history (Affleck and Steed 2001). The adoption agency where you were adopted probably has some information about your biological parents' background, but you most likely do not have access to these records. Even if you do have access to this information it does not mean it is current. Personal situations change throughout one's life. The medical information needs to be updated regularly. This is not always the case in adoptions. Your birth parents might have inadvertently forgotten to update their records. Maybe your birth parents or your adoptive parents moved and forget to send a forwarding address to the adoption agency. This makes it difficult for you to get accurate health information when it is needed.

Another common medical situation with adoptees is dreading going to the doctor. Do you resent being asked about your parents' medical history? Your response is always the same and then there is that moment of silence where the doctor is trying to figure out what to say back to you. The doctor never responds and then keeps on asking questions as if you were a typical patient with a complete medical background.

> *Normally I became very tense when the doctor would ask about my family history of diseases. I usually just made something up or gave no information at all. It was such a great feeling to be able to answer the doctor's questions truthfully that first time after I got my complete medical background. I was surprised how much not having my family history had affected me.*

Challenge. Do you strongly believe you have the right to your medical background? Do you worry that you might inherit a disease that could be preventable? Do you frequently wonder if some quirky trait you have came from one of your birth parents? Do you wonder if you are genetically programmed to be skinny or overweight? What specific information are you seeking? What will you do with this information once you get it? Will you change your lifestyle? If you cannot get this information from the social service agency, are you willing to undergo blood tests or medical procedures to answer your questions? Do you know of any doctors who will help you? Will your parents consent to the tests being done?

Solution. Fortunately, your parents may be able to get access to the information you are seeking relatively easily. Many social service agencies keep medical backgrounds on their birth parents. In some cases it is just a fax or e-mail away from your parents and you. If this is not possible in your case, medical technology may be able to provide you with the questions to your answers. Simple blood tests can provide lots of information about your health. Other more invasive procedures can provide even more detailed information if you are willing to undergo them.

Plan. Determine exactly what type of information you want to know; blood type, family diseases, cancer risks or alcohol and drug abuse history. Explain to your parents why this information is important for you to know. Ask your parents to help you contact the social service agency. Place a deadline on your plan so you will follow through. If your parents are unable to get your medical history and you still want the information, you can talk to your parents about making an appointment with your family doctor to design a plan for checking your health risks.

Transracial Issues. If your ethnicity is different from your parents' ethnicity this presents additional challenges for you as an adopted teenager. You have known since a young age that you did not share the same skin color as your parents. It was just accepted as part of your family. You were colorblind. As you grew up you probably started noticing strangers making insensitive comments to you and your parents. The stares and questions by others became more noticeable throughout elementary school. By now you probably have several well-scripted responses to these comments and awkward stares.

Unfortunately, race issues will not get easier during adolescence for you. In fact, these issues will probably become more difficult. You may find social decisions difficult to make as you grow older. One such time is when you begin to have crushes or start dating. Let's say you are African American and your parents are Caucasian. How would your parents react if you dated an African American? Your parents are obviously very accepting of you as their African American child, but it may be more difficult for them to accept someone outside their Caucasian race as your boyfriend. On the other hand, how would you feel dating a Caucasian? There are no simple solutions to these issues.

You may face direct racial discrimination within your own extended family. Examples of racism take the form of rude comments and exclusion from family activities. Relatives who make you feel as if you are not part of the family based on your skin color may very well be racist. This type of behavior generally is known to occur among the older generations of the family. Others in your family may just be against transracial adoption. Their ignorance in transracial adoptions tends to make them act this way.

Religion may become an important issue in your family, too. If you were adopted from China, you can almost guarantee your birth parents were not Catholic. Likewise, if you have blond hair and blue eyes you will be different from the majority of the members in your Jewish synagogue. These differences are undeniable and make you stand out from the rest of the group.

Again, these differences become very noticeable during adolescence when fitting in is so important. The result may be a decreased interest in doing religious activities. Your parents will be more understanding if you explain your reasons for not wanting to go on that weekend retreat rather than let them think you are straying from your morals.

Your ethnicity will become even more apparent to you as you leave your parents' home for college or the "real" world. Let's assume you are of Korean descent raised in a Caucasian home. Your whole life you have been raised with Caucasian ideals and Caucasian relatives and friends. When you go to college you may feel compelled to choose between Caucasian and Korean social circles. For the first time in your life you will have the option to get to know people from your home country and who look very similar to you.

You may want to take this opportunity to explore for yourself firsthand your ancestral roots. You also may find this opportunity to get to know others similar to you exciting but scary. If you feel compelled to choose between the two groups, no right or wrong decision can be made. It is perfectly understandable if you choose to remain with people similar to the ones you knew throughout childhood. If you choose to experiment with your cultural group, you will learn a lot about yourself and have remarkable experiences to tell your old friends and family.

The experiences of being a transracial adoptee may help you to be more accepting of other people who are different. You may see that you have a variety of friends. You may also notice that you are able to get along with all kinds of people, not just people like yourself. Individuals who are able to mix with different types of people find themselves living a very interesting and successful life.

> **Challenge.** Do you experience discrimination from people inside your family, in your neighborhood or at school? Are you having trouble finding dates at school? Do you wish you knew more about the country you came from and your ancestors?

> **Solution**. Unfortunately you can't change what other people think or feel about you, but you can change how you respond to those who are discriminating against you. You can use humor when someone says something rude to you. You can completely ignore their comments, too. You can also come up with a short and simple statement that says you are not going to waste your valuable time responding to their rude comments. If you cannot think of anything to say, try these suggestions by Fred Frankel (1996),
>> "So what?"
>> "Can't you think of anything else to say?"
>> "And your point is…"
> Another more complicated issue is dating. Define your comfort zone and what you believe to be your parents' comfort zone with regards to dating someone of your race or a different race. Are the comfort zones compatible? If you and your parents do not see eye-to-eye on dating, can a compromise be reached? Maybe if your parents got to know your friend better they wouldn't be so against the two of you dating.

Getting to know your ancestral background is easy to accomplish. A quick Internet search is sure to give you lots of information about your birth country. While you are on the Internet, check out local restaurants and museums to visit along with upcoming festivals and events that focus on your ethnicity.

Plan. List all the racial comments you can think of that have been said to you. Determine how you will react if someone says them to you in the future. Figure out what your response will be. Don't forget to rehearse them aloud so they seem natural.

If you and your parents have not talked about dating yet, this might be a good time to introduce the topic to them. Chances are they have already thought about it and are waiting for you to bring it to their attention first. Present some potential scenarios to see how they react. If your parents are not comfortable with the individual you would like to date, try inviting that person over for a study session or to work on a project. You can also invite that person of interest over to your house along with some of your friends that your parents do like. Once your parents get to know this person, they might not mind if you two start dating.

In regards to finding ethnic information, setting a time to search the Internet is a great place to start. You should find ethnic restaurants, museums and festivals close to your home. Once you have all of the information you need, ask your parents to help you plan visits to these places either with them or a friend. Be sure to include how you plan on getting there, how much money you need, and how you will earn it. This sort of planning shows you are responsible and can be trusted.

Control Issues. You may feel people have been controlling your life since before you were even born. It seems everyone has been making decisions on how you should be raised, even people you have never met. Now that you have reached adolescence, you are ready to start taking control of your life while your parents give up some of the control they have had over you for years. You may find your past and present control issues coming together all at once resulting in more arguments with your parents. You are demanding more independence while your parents are reluctant to give you as much as you want.

Some parents believe that adopted children are more likely to have behavior problems than nonadopted children. If your parents believe this stereotype, they will be even more reluctant as to how much control they give up to you. Your parents may fear that you have a genetic tendency toward delinquent behaviors. For instance, if your birth father was in jail when you were born, your parents may believe you are more likely to follow in his footsteps if you are not watched carefully.

In some cases, not necessarily yours, it seems the more parents try to control their teenager the more out of control their teenager becomes, at least from a parent's perspective. Disobeying and arguing with your parents is a common reaction to being controlled, especially as a teenager. Being able to separate from your parents without getting into too much trouble is important in helping you become your own person.

If you are having difficulty getting your parents to give you more control, then showing responsibility for even the smallest parts of your life will demonstrate to your parents you are responsible. Responsible behaviors on your part will likely result in less control and more independence for you. With responsibility comes freedom.

> **Challenge**. Do your parents try to control who your friends are? Do your parents always assume you are getting into trouble with your friends? Do your parents demand to know every little detail of your life? Do your parents schedule every minute of your life with activities so you don't have time to spend with your friends? Do you feel you have no privacy at all?

> **Solution**. If you want your parents to relax about your whereabouts and activities, you are going to have to show them that they can trust you. This means if you have gotten into trouble for doing illegal activities or taking excessive risks that endanger yourself or others, then you have a lot of work to do to change their opinions

of you. Showing responsibility and gaining trust means keeping your room cleaned and doing chores without being asked, keeping up on your homework, and getting decent grades, telling your parents where you are going and who you are going out with and then coming home on time, talking to them in a respectful tone of voice, not talking back and even spending time with them doing activities they enjoy.

Plan. If you have a bad reputation with your parents, you need to figure out how you can repair the damage that has been done. If you violate curfew frequently, then try coming home early or at least on time. If you have to be told constantly to do your chores, try doing them before you are supposed to have them done. Do you see the pattern here? Make a list of all the ways you can be more responsible and follow through with them. Remember, the more trouble you have gotten into, the more you are going to have to work at gaining back the trust from your parents.

Searching for Meaning. Every adolescent searches for his or her meaning in life at some point in time. This is normal teenage behavior. If you are adopted, the search for meaning takes on a whole new perspective. You have probably asked yourself why you are going through what you are and what you are supposed to learn from your experiences.

> It's all these issues. Maybe this is a life lesson I have to work out on my part.

You may be questioning if God or some other higher power even exists. You might wonder if life is a random set of events or organized chaos. You might wonder if this is really happening to you, especially if you watch science fiction movies. Your life may even seem like a science fiction movie where you were not really born but exist in some other world. You may feel as if somehow you just appeared on this earth. You have no birth certificate, no pregnancy stories, no birth stories, and no pictures.

I would ask myself if my life was real or if it was in my imagination. I thought maybe I would wake up some day somewhere else and this life would just be a dream.

You might have also imagined the outcome if a different set of parents had been selected for you or if your biological parents raised you instead of placing you for adoption. You might be wondering if you would still have the same personality, the same hobbies, the same talents, the same type of friends, and the same clothing and hair styles.

I used to think a lot about how different my life would have been if my biological parents could have figured out how to make it all work. Maybe I would be living in the Southwest on a ranch instead of in a Midwestern town. Then I would wonder what would have happened if I ended up being adopted by a famous couple. I wondered how my life would be different. In fact, I still think about it today.

Challenge. What life questions do you ask yourself? Do they reflect a deeper meaning to understand the events of your life or are they typical of your peers? What is your view of religion? What issues do you feel deeply passionate about; family, teen pregnancy, drug abuse?

Solution. Writing your thoughts in a journal will help you understand why you are thinking certain thoughts and feeling certain feelings. Unless you are an avid writer, this activity might take some practice to get everything down on paper that you are feeling. The more you write, the more you will understand. Visiting the library and reading about your interests helps, too. If you are trying to figure out why you are who you are, check out some books or articles about twins who have been separated at birth and later reunited. Or if you are interested in why you are with your particular family today, check out books about teen pregnancy and adoption options. You may gain some insights about why you have the parents that you do.

Plan. Find a notebook or journal you can use to write down your thoughts. Schedule a time when you will not be interrupted. A good place for this might be the library where you can also check out some books on adoption, twin studies or whatever interests you. Schedule a time to search the Internet for other good books, articles or interviews on your interests.

Something Is Missing. Emptiness is a feeling that cannot be measured and is hard to understand if you have never felt it. Emptiness can be a powerful feeling that will affect many aspects of your life. You may feel like you are constantly searching for that one person, activity, award or job that will make you a complete person.

Emptiness cannot be satisfied through extracurricular activities, work, intimate friends, peers, hobbies or your family. Emptiness is a dull feeling like something is missing, but you cannot figure out what it is no matter how hard you try. You may keep searching for that one activity or that one boyfriend to fill that empty space inside of you. People on the outside may describe you as indecisive. This may just be a personality trait, but it could very well be the result of a need to fill that emptiness inside of you.

> It did not matter what I succeeded at, there was always a void that needed to be filled. I always felt something was missing. I think this is why I always feel the need to over-accomplish. I believed I could fill up the emptiness with awards and recognition, but it never worked.

You may also feel as if you are unconnected, especially if you do not know anything about your biological parents. You cannot see the resemblances between you and your siblings or you and your grandparents. You may have a baby book from your adoptive parents that describes every milestone in great detail from the time you were adopted, but you may feel this is not enough. You need to connect with a concrete, biological relative.

Your friends and family may be confused how you can feel unconnected. They cannot imagine how you can feel unconnected when you
have family and friends all around you. They have connections to their
genetic past. They have always been connected to others around them
biologically, so they do not know what unconnected feels like.

This may not make sense to you right now. That is okay. Just
remember if you do start having these feelings, it is part of our human
nature to want to connect with our blood relatives. In fact, an undeniable bond exists between a mother and her child. If that child is
adopted, the bond that was established early on does not disappear
completely. This bond may be negative or positive, but a bond still
formed. This probably explains why people who search for their biological parents start with finding their birth mother first.

Unfortunately, there is no quick remedy to feeling empty or unconnected. This is one instance where you just have to learn to recognize
these feelings as being present and accept them. You can hope that
some day you will get the chance to have your questions answered that
created this emptiness or your feelings of being unconnected. Some
adoptees that have had their questions answered explain that a certain
amount of emptiness remains. On the other hand, some feel a sense of
completeness or calming in their lives.

> *Once I got all of the answers to my questions, a great sense of relief
> swept over me. I felt I could go on with my life. It seemed like every-
> thing else fell into place after that.*

Challenge. Do you always feel like something is missing from
your life? Do you feel like you just don't belong anywhere? Do you
always feel restless? Do you keep trying activities only to find out
they are not as interesting as you thought?

Solution. Try to figure out when these feelings of restlessness or
unconnectedness occur. Do they only occur during major events
in your life? Do these feelings surface frequently during school, at

home or with peers? Do these feelings show up during certain activities like church, family reunions or sleepovers with your friends? Keeping a detailed journal noting the time of day, the activity and the people involved will likely show a trend. You could just be bored or not challenged enough at school if these feelings occur mostly in that setting. If these feelings occur generally during family get-togethers, maybe you are noticing differences between yourself and your adoptive relatives. If these feelings occur all the time, you could be experiencing depression or having attention problems. Depression and ADD/ADHD are suspected of being genetically passed along the family tree. This might be the perfect opportunity to ask and receive medical background information from your parents.

Plan. Create an organized system to note your observations. You can use a notebook, journal or note cards. Record the date, the time, who you are with and what happened right before you started getting this empty feeling. Plan on keeping track of your feelings for quite a while. This may take months depending how frequently you feel something is missing. Take all of your information and show it to your parents. When they see all of the work you have done, they will be more willing to help you search for what is missing.

Fear of Rejection and Abandonment. Adopted teens usually form strong opinions on how their birth parents should have handled an unexpected pregnancy. Some believe their birth parents should have tried to work out their situation without resorting to adoption. Others believe their birth parents felt an obligation to provide a better life for their child by placing the child for adoption. These two groups of teens will have different views of rejection. Again, every person feels adoption issues differently. Your views will depend on your personal social beliefs combined with the facts of your adoption.

Abandonment has been used for many decades to describe children who have been placed for adoption. If you can change your perceptions for a moment, you will see abandonment is not really the proper word to describe birth parents that place their children with other families. Your birth mother did not abandon you. She made a plan to have someone else, more capable than herself, take care of you. This is hardly abandoning you. Even if your birth mother anonymously left you at a train station or airport, she did not abandon you. She was making sure that you would be quickly found and placed with another family in a better environment.

For instance, birth mothers in China have three choices when confronted with an unplanned pregnancy; she can hide her pregnancy and then "abandon" her child, face abortion or suffer severe financial consequences from the government. These birth mothers who choose life for their unborn child risk harsh consequences. After she gives birth, she must leave this child in such a way that the child cannot be traced to her or her family. Many of the infants that have been adopted in the United States from China were found in busy markets, heavily traveled areas, and in doorways of businesses. These mothers put their infants in places so they would be found quickly. They knew this was the only way for their infant to have a chance at life. These mothers clearly did not abandon their children.

However, the fear of rejection can be real for you, even if you understand the circumstances surrounding your birth. You may express fear of rejection in several different ways. You may have difficulty establishing trusting relationships with others, fear failure in your parents' eyes, have difficulty disagreeing with your parents (yes, some teenagers do have this problem) or fear leaving home.

Hidden feelings may make you think that if your birth parents rejected you, then there must be something wrong with you. This hidden feeling will surface when you do not want to expose your personal details to others. You may fear they will not like you and reject you, too. Instead, you build a wall around your life to protect yourself from rejection.

> *I've always had this problem getting close to friends. I feel the need to keep a safe distance between others so as to protect myself from being rejected. I'm afraid if they get to know the real me, they will not want to be my friends.*

If you grew up being told you were specially chosen, then you may feel you have to live up to some high expectations set out by your parents. This can create a tremendous amount of pressure for you. You may wonder what will happen if you do not live up to their expectations. Will they abandon you like your birth mother did? If your parents told you the "especially chosen" story, they just wanted you to know that you belonged in the family. Rest assured, they will not reject you if you do not meet their expectations.

Fear of rejection can surface for you when you argue with your parents. Even though arguing with parents can be described as typical teenage behavior, you may think your parents will "give you up" just like your biological parents did many years ago. The result is you avoid confrontation with your parents. Your feelings have no way of escaping and will eventually build up and boil over. You may say something that you don't really mean to your parents. Your parents will be shocked and puzzled by your outburst. On the other hand, you may store up these feelings until you become ill. This is not good either.

This fear of rejection can show up when you are getting ready to move away from home or go to college. You may feel anxious when someone asks you about your future plans. You may feel you have been rejected once by your biological parents and by leaving the comfort of your home you will be rejected again. If it makes you feel better, it is perfectly normal for teenagers to fear leaving the security of their parents' home to enter the world on their own, adopted or not.

Regardless of the source of your fear of rejection, you have to deal with it in order to have satisfying relationships later in life. This means if you want to have close friendships or a serious girlfriend or boy-friend, you will need to deal with your fear of rejection now.

Challenge. Do you have a hard time forming relationships? Do you fear others will not like you once they know you are adopted? Are you afraid your parents will forget about you when you become an adult?

Solution. Teenagers naturally fear some rejection during adolescence. This is normal. If you're adopted, you may feel this fear more intensely. There is a way to resolve these feelings. Instead of focusing on your fear of being rejected by others, think about all of the positive qualities you have that you can share with others. Spend your energy trying to develop these positive qualities instead of sabotaging them through your fears.

Plan. Brainstorm all of your good traits and talents. Don't stop with just a couple. Once you have a decent list, think of all the ways to use your good qualities. Check out local volunteer activities and clubs that would appreciate your personality and skills (museums, local animal shelters, Key Club, library, and literacy programs are a few examples). Try to put some extra time into nurturing a promising relationship by focusing on what you can give to the other person.

Anger. Do people avoid talking to you about your experiences with being adopted because you become very emotional and go on and on about your parents, your birth parents or how unfair the social system is to adoptees? These feelings of anger can generally be traced to how you feel your birth parents handled your adoption, how you feel your adoptive parents, treat you, or how the social system has worked or not worked for you. The following quote from an adoptee shows how she feels about her entire adoption experience, not just one part of being adopted. Unfortunately, many adoptees express the same feelings about their adoptions as well. Simply put,

There's so much anger in me.

Anger toward your birth parents may become significant right now as you are trying to make sense out of the world. Giving you to strangers does not make sense, even if you do dearly love your adoptive parents. You may be asking yourself how someone could just give their child to someone else. You want to know what kind of person would do that sort of thing. You may also be wondering if you are like your biological parent and if you would do that, too.

> *Looking back I was pretty lucky. There were a lot of relatives and love in our family, but I spent a great deal of my time growing up trying to hide my past. I didn't want anybody to know I wasn't wanted. I was angry that my birth father was not willing to help my birth mother keep us together as a family. I was angry that I was given away like someone would give away an old pair of jeans. Living with these feelings generated a lot of anger toward everybody in my life, including those who raised me.*

Your anger can surge from a need for an explanation, which you are not getting. It is natural to want to know the circumstances of your birth. You probably want to know why you were placed for adoption and who made the decision. You want to know the details of your birth, how your birth mother felt when you were placed with your new family and how she dealt with not being able to raise you herself.

> *I finally had my chance to ask my birth father all of the questions I had ever had while growing up. He was the one person who held all the answers. I finally had the opportunity of a lifetime to ask him. After all those years with no information he told me that he would tell me one day but this was not the right time. I was so angry with him. I'm not sure that I have ever been that angry with anybody my whole entire life.*

You may be angry with your parents for not providing you with the information you desperately want to know. Maybe they refused to help you get this information. Maybe they will not talk to you about your adoption at all. Maybe you feel they are keeping some big secret from you. These circumstances certainly can provoke anger inside you.

> *I have always wondered why I was placed for adoption. My mom has always told me that my biological mother was young and that her family was wealthy and that her family would disown her if she did not place the baby up for adoption. I am not sure how my mother knows all this information. I have always wondered if it was correct information.*

Maybe your parents have tried too hard to make you fit in with their family style. They may indulge your every wish. They devote every minute in making you feel happy, regardless of what they really want. In this instance, your individuality has been ignored. You can be angry with them for not respecting you as an individual person.

Perhaps you are angry with your parents for always imposing their hobbies or talents on you when you have no interest in their activities. Suppose you are very artistic. You love to write and paint. Your parents, on the other hand, have pushed you into sports to fulfill their dream of coaching their child's team. This can make you angry, too.

You may be angry at the social system. If you are not happy living with your parents, you may blame the social system for placing you with your particular family. If you are trying to find information about your biological parents, you may be angry with the laws and the agencies that you deal with in your search. You may be angry that strangers know your personal information, but you are not allowed to see your own file.

> *I am angry at the social system. I feel they have no right to keep biological/genetic information from me. I feel that I have the right to know if I may end up with respiratory diseases, breast cancer or muscular disorders. I have the right to know if my children are at high risk for these diseases. I am angry that I have to explain at every doctor's appoint-*

ment that I do not know the maternal history for my children. I am angry that the social system feels the need to protect one person over multiple people.

If you were placed in an abusive or neglected home, you most likely have angry feelings toward your birth parents, your adoptive parents and the social system. Perhaps a divorce occurred, your parents could not give you the attention you deserved or your parents could not financially afford you, then you might be very angry that you were placed in potentially worse conditions than if you had stayed with your birth mother. Even the social system failed you. You have a right to be angry. An adoptee who was placed in similar circumstances expresses her reaction to the anger she felt by saying,

I always felt unloved. Sometimes I just blocked it out so I didn't have to feel.

It may seem the whole world is against you at times. If you let your anger build inside you, you may be surprised when you inadvertently tell your parents they can't make you do anything because they are not your "real" parents. You may tell them you wish you could live with your "real" parents instead of them. Even if you don't actually tell your parents these feelings, you have probably thought them on occasion. Dealing with your anger now will save you from a lot of emotional problems later in life.

Challenge. Do you feel like your birth parents "gave" you away? Do you get upset with your parents for not giving you information about your adoption or birth parents? Do you feel neglected by your adoptive parents? Do you feel your life could have been better if you were not placed for adoption or if you were placed with a different family?

Solution. Make a list of what makes you angry. Decide what you have to do to make your anger go away. You might have to tell your parents or your birth parents how you feel. Decide if you will write a letter or talk to the people directly. Even if you can't talk to the people who make you angry or you do not have an address to put on the envelope, just writing about your anger will make you feel better.

Does your situation require forgiveness? You are not saying what happened to you is okay. You are saying that you are tired of this issue controlling your life. You are deciding to not let the anger interfere with growing up any longer. You can experience forgiveness by writing a letter to the person you are angry at or telling them in person. You can also just decide you are not going to think about it any longer. Whenever you start to feel angry, remind yourself of the decision not to let it affect your life anymore. If you try not letting the anger bother you or writing a letter and that does not work, you probably need to confront the person directly.

Plan. Set aside a time to write your letter or talk to the person or persons directly. Determine how you will act if you start to feel angry again. You will know you have resolved your anger when you can talk about the problem without getting upset.

Loss. You may have a difficult time understanding how you can feel the loss of your birth parents when you never knew them. This is especially true if you have loving and caring parents or a generally happy life. If you are having a hard time understanding how you can feel this way, imagine someone on the outside trying to understand how you can feel this way. How many times have you heard how lucky you are to have been adopted by such a good family? If you are transracially adopted you have probably heard how nice it was of your parents to rescue you from such a hard life. This doesn't help you with your feelings of loss. These comments may only complicate matters further for you by making you feel guilty for grieving the loss of your birth parents.

Challenge. Do you often feel you will lose your adoptive family? Do you feel a sense of loss from not knowing your birth parents?

Solution. The first step in dealing with your feelings of loss is to express just what you feel you have lost. After you can put words to your feelings, then you are ready to move forward. Putting an end to these feelings means looking forward instead of dwelling on the past. When you start to have these feelings again, notice the feelings and then tell yourself to refocus on the future.

Plan. Grab a piece of paper or a good friend who is also a good listener. Express all of your feelings about what you have lost. After you have gotten that out of your system, write down some short-term and long-term goals you want to accomplish. Whenever you start feeling sad, remind yourself of your goals.

Identity. Scientists have known for a long time that genes play an important role in determining our hair color, eye color, blood type, and other such characteristics. Scientific discoveries are being made every day that explains how our genes are passed down from generation to generation to influence certain diseases, body types, and personality traits. However, no one has figured out just how much influence our genes play in determining who we are as individuals. We do not know what portion of our identity is shaped by our life experiences versus our genetic makeup.

Genetic advancements are thrilling to many people, adoptees especially. On the other hand, scientific advancements may confuse you even more while you are trying to figure out your own place in the world. You probably wonder to what extent your genes and family environment have affected you. You may wonder which of your traits you have no control over and which ones you can change.

Life experiences, along with genetics, do shape who you are today and will become in the future. However, you do not need biological parents to figure out who you are right now. You can answer this question yourself. You already know who you are by taking a careful look inside yourself. You are the person that you are. No one can change you. You are a product of your biology and environment. Your genes provide your framework and your environment shapes the rest of you.

When you seek information about your birth parents in helping you identify yourself, you are just seeking labels. Those labels do not change who you are. Let's assume your biological parents eventually got married and had more children. Now let's assume they did not get married and have never seen each other since your birth. Regardless of what happened to your birth parents, you are still you. It doesn't matter whether your birth mother has red hair, brown hair or blond hair, you have not changed.

Now you may be more likely to inherit certain traits. You cannot change those traits but those traits have been part of you since birth. Adoptees and birth parents who reunite often find striking similarities despite living completely different lives. However, there are also just as many, if not more, differences between you and your birth parents. You don't need biological roots to define yourself. With or without the knowledge of those roots, you are still you.

If you want to find your identity, ask yourself what makes you the person you are right now. Are you funny, outgoing, introverted, loud, hyperactive, caring, highly motivated or relaxed? Maybe you are a little of all of them depending on who you are with at the time. What are your hobbies and interests? Your answers will provide clues as to your identity.

Your identity is made up of stable characteristics that are naturally part of you. You can choose to develop the traits to become what you think you want to be like. For example, if you feel you have a special talent for helping others, you can explore hobbies or interests that require a person with caring traits. Medicine and teaching would be examples of such careers. If you love animals you might be inspired to volunteer at an animal shelter caring for the homeless pets. Those traits are characteristics of you that nobody can change. You will always be caring no matter what your circumstances.

The same can be true for specific talents. Maybe you are very athletic. You would have likely been athletic even if you lived with people other than your adoptive parents. There are some people who are not athletic but would like to be. If you are one of these people, you may work hard and succeed or decide your time and talents could be put to better use elsewhere. The bottom line is that is just part of who you are. You do not need biological parents to tell you that you are or are not athletic.

However, be careful not to mistake applying labels to yourself in determining your identity. Religious affiliation, social class, peer group status (brain, jock, geek), club membership, and choice of extracurricular activities are examples of labels teens use to describe themselves. You may describe yourself as a student, cheerleader, artist, and popular. On the other hand, you may define yourself as an illegitimate child given away by your birth parents. You are placing labels on yourself. If you choose labels that have negative meanings, you are restricting your potential in many areas. Focusing your energies on your natural talents and positive traits will make a strong foundation for your identity. You will know who you are and in what direction your life should go.

Do not be afraid to experiment with different hobbies and interests. Do not be afraid to quit these activities if you are not enjoying them. The only way to find out who you are is to experiment by playing different parts. When you find yourself very interested in a specific topic, stop and take a mental note of it. Better yet, write it down for later use.

For instance, let's say you are dissecting a frog in biology class, the one class you manage to ace without even trying. You think this is one of the coolest things you have ever done in school. Maybe you find yourself at the local science store buying other preserved animals to dissect. In fact, you remember when you were younger you used to study dead insects under your microscope. When you put all the little pieces of information together, you can see a bigger picture developing. Biology seems to be something you are naturally drawn toward. When you start exploring career options, you can take this information you have collected throughout your teen years and explore possibilities in medicine, science or research.

Be careful not to limit yourself to just a couple of interests, because you will play many roles in life. Today you play a student and captain of the football team. Next year you may be the class president. One day you may be a parent, a corporate executive, and little league coach. Chances are you will be attracted to these roles because of who you are and the traits you have. You have always shown your strength as a leader. Your leadership qualities are part of your stable identity. Your roles have changed, but you have not.

Don't let labels restrict what you can become. Find your strengths and talents to become the best person you can become. Your genetic tendencies as well as your family environment do influence your behavior, thinking, interests, and ultimately guide you down the path of life. However, you determine your outcome and your happiness, not anyone else. You write your own life story, so you might as well make it good.

Your identity will change throughout your teenage years. You may not be able to describe yourself until your late teens or early twenties. Some people, adopted or not, do not know who they are until their thirties. Some professionals tell us that adolescence is not defined by age but rather when the person is done searching for their identity. By that definition some people never leave adolescence!

Challenge. Are you completely confused about who you are and where you are going in your life? Most teenagers are at some point during adolescence. Are you having a hard time finding your strengths and talents? Do you wish you could uncover the real you?

Solution. The good news is this is the most fun part of being a teenager. Adults expect you to change your interests, activities, hobbies, and career goals often. You can experiment with as many different types of roles as you want. In fact, the more you try, the better it is for you.

Plan. Make a list of all the activities, hobbies or clubs you would like to try. Figure out where to find the information related to your interests. Teachers and school counselors are great resources for finding out this information. Also, try the Internet and local phone book. Determine how much it will cost and who is going to pay for it. You also have to have a way to and from your activities. Once you have all the details, put your plans in your schedule book.

Sibling Rivalry. Sibling rivalry takes on a new definition when some kids are adopted and some kids are the natural offspring of the parents. If you are one of the growing numbers of adopted teens who also shares a house with siblings who are genetically related to the parents, you know the problems that can happen in this type of family.

You have probably felt countless times that your siblings were being treated better than you. Teenagers have always questioned their parents' acts of favoritism toward siblings. Preferential treatment has always been an issue in families with more than one child. If you are adopted additional feelings come into play. You may have moments when you feel your parents do not love you as much as they love your brothers and sisters.

From your siblings' viewpoint, they may very well feel that you are treated better than they are because you are adopted. If your parents told you that you were specially chosen, then these comments can be proof that your parents do in fact give you special treatment, at least from your siblings' viewpoint.

Challenge. Do you constantly fight with your siblings? Do you feel you are treated worse than your siblings?

Solution. If you fight with your siblings a lot, maybe you need some space and time away from each other, especially if you share a room. Create a special place in the house that is just yours. This could be a large closet, corner in the basement or practically anywhere. With the permission of your parents, tell everyone that it is your space and no one should enter without your permission.

If you feel your parents treat you worse than your siblings, maybe there is a reason. Are you at an age where you are not allowed to do the same things your older siblings get to do? Are you the older sibling in a home where more is expected of you because you are older? Do you do things that get you into trouble? If any of these apply to you, then you must earn the respect of your parents. As mentioned before, the more reasons you give them to trust you, the better they will treat you. This means pulling your weight, and sometimes more, around the house. Again, doing homework and chores without being asked is always a good place to start.

Plan. Decide if you need a space of your own. If you do, work with your parents to find a space that you can claim as your own. The only thing left to do is to decorate it in a way that says it is your space. Be creative!

Now if you want to be treated better, then you have to decide what you can do around the house that will show you deserve more respect. Make a list of the ways you are going to prove your respectability. Schedule times to complete these activities and then start doing them. Your parents are sure to notice the change in your maturity level.

Peers. Responding to peers' comments about why your real parents did not keep you or their unending questions about what it must feel like being adopted puts you in an uncomfortable position sometimes. The unwelcome comments from others can certainly touch a sensitive nerve in you, especially when you hit the teen years.

When your friends or peers at school start asking personal questions you would rather not talk about, try to remember their comments and questions is their way of expressing confusion about adoption. Most likely their remarks are not intended to be hurtful. Sometimes people are curious but do not know how to ask questions, so they appear to be rude and insensitive toward you. Inviting people to ask questions can help dispel some of the myths around adoption. You also have the right to tell them that such questions are personal and you would rather not discuss them right at that moment. That should politely but firmly put an end to the conversation.

On the other hand, people have been known to make mean comments on purpose. Have you ever been in an argument with a friend only to hear them say your real mother didn't even want you? Have your friends ever told you that your parents are not your real parents so they cannot make you do anything you do not want to? Remarks such as these are sure to happen at some point while growing up.

> **Challenge.** What types of comments make you upset? Why do these comments make you upset? Do the comments bring up issues already discussed such as being different, loss, fear of rejection or anger?

> **Solution.** If previous issues come to the surface when others make comments, go back to that section and see how to solve the problem. Otherwise, invite others to ask questions. Most people cannot comprehend what it is like being adopted.

> **Plan**. Determine how you will respond when others make comments about your adoption. Rehearse your comments aloud so they seem natural. Decide if you need to review previous sections to solve any unresolved issues.

Still Need Help? If any items on the following list apply to you, find someone to help you as soon as possible. A school counselor, nurse or teacher can help you if you are not comfortable talking to your parents. The important point is you get the help you need now!

- Sudden problems at school with grades or truancy
- Sudden problems with peers
- Feel the need to use drugs or alcohol
- Feel emotionally unavailable to the people closest to you
- Thoughts of suicide—seek help immediately
- Stealing
- Feeling hopeless
- Difficulty concentrating
- Sleep difficulties
- Unusually tired

National Certified Crisis Hotline	800-784-2433 (800-SUICIDE)
Boys Town Hotline	800-448-3000
National Youth Crisis Hotline	800-621-4000

Chapter Two

Adoptive Parents

Most adoptive parents are extremely committed to helping their children grow up healthy and happy. In fact, adoptive parents are given significantly more professional training on how to raise children than most other mothers and fathers in the United States today. These parents appreciate having their adoptive children a part of their family, even when their teen refuses to speak to them.

Despite all of the parental training and counseling, adoptive parents do have difficulties with certain aspects of raising adopted children. Ironically, adoptive parents feel many of the same feelings that adoptees feel as the result of adoption. Adoptive parents may experience several of these feelings or only one or two. It is important to remember that each parent has their own set of beliefs, expectations, and feelings about adoption. Sometimes the parents within the family differ on adoption issues, too.

Being Different. If your parents are like most parents, they talk with their neighbors and friends about the things you are doing that worries them. They are curious to know if your behavior is similar to their teenager's behaviors. They wonder if their friends are having the same misunderstandings and struggles with their teen as they are with you. They want advice from parents who are going through similar situations. Although, your parents probably have a hard time finding other families with adopted teens in them.

Just as you feel being adopted is different from your peers, your parents sometimes feel they are different from other parents. Your parents may feel that other parents do not understand your family situation. The issues your parents seek answers to are basically the same issues other families face, but your family situation is more complicated when you throw adoption into the family dynamics.

For instance, it would be impossible for the nonadoptive family next door to understand why your parents are struggling with the decision of how much information to give you about your biological parents. They could not possibly grasp all of the consequences, whether good or bad, that could happen to your family. Your neighbors most likely have never even considered whether their child might want to live with someone else. The idea of spending a summer on the other side of the world looking for their child's relatives has probably never been imagined either.

Just like with you, well-meaning people may react in ways to your family that puts your parents in awkward positions that further show how your family is different from other families. For example, if you are transracially adopted your parents have had to endure the stares of others just as you have tolerated. They may have had to respond to racial remarks. They feel the anxiety that others place on them in trying to figure out if you are related or a neighborhood friend. These experiences can be quite uncomfortable for your parents as well as you.

Your parents may experience comments from other people when talking about your adoption. People may pry into their private lives as to the circumstances that brought your family together. The more questions asked, the more your parents realize how different your family situation is from families around them. Again, not all parents react like this, but some do take this invasion of privacy personally.

Your parents may be affected more deeply than you by these questions and comments, because being a parent brings on strong feelings of providing protection for you. When someone makes a negative comment about you or makes your parents feel uncomfortable, they instinctively become defensive. Your parents want you to fit in just as much as you want to fit in with the people around you.

Control Issues. As you begin testing your limits with your parents, you may feel your parents trying to control your actions to an even greater extent. Reasons do exist for their overly controlling behavior. They may believe you are destined to act a certain way. Perhaps, they may be experiencing unsettled feelings about your emerging sexual maturity. Fear of losing you may also account for their unusual behaviors.

Your parents may interpret your resistance to authority and following rules as a genetic problem instead of normal adolescent behavior. Your parents may feel they need to control you so you do not get involved in some unavoidable self-destructive behaviors. For instance, if your birth mother had a history of substance abuse, they may fear you will too. Your parents might be asking you a lot of questions about your friends and activities out of their own fears. Of course, parental interference in your life should be normal to some degree. You would not want complete pushovers for parents either.

Your parents may be uncomfortable with your developing sexuality, especially if your birth parents were young teenagers. They may fear you will follow the same path by becoming a teenage parent, too. Their reaction is to control you even more now that you are older. On the other hand, maybe they are reminded of their own fertility problems. If those issues have not been resolved for them, then your adolescence may bring those painful memories of trying to have a baby to the surface again.

Your parents may become confused about how to properly parent you. They may not be able to tell the difference between normal adolescent development from adoption-related concerns. Their reaction is to do nothing or try to become more involved in your life. If they do nothing, then it seems as if they do not care. If they try to control you more, it will seem like they are smothering you. Both decisions result in conflicts between you and your parents.

If control issues seem to be a particular concern for you and your parents, don't worry. You will eventually become your own separate person. The process may take longer and you will have more hurdles to cross along the way, but it will happen. Once again, proving yourself as a responsible teen may convince your parents to relax their rules a bit.

Now if your parents have totally given up on keeping track of what you are doing, you probably find yourself in verbally or physically abusive arguments with them. You may run away or threaten to run away. Likewise, your parents may threaten or actually throw you out of the house. These threats are telling you there is a serious problem that cannot be explained by normal adolescent behavior. Maybe you just need to connect with your birth mother. Maybe you are having serious problems dealing with issues of rejection or loss. Maybe your problem is not even related to adoption at all. Only a professional counselor can help you and your family. If this sounds like your family, refer back to Chapter One to see where to get help or advance to Chapter Six to see how to talk to your parents.

Searching for Meaning. Your parents may often wonder what would have happened to them if you had not come into their lives. They may try to imagine a life without the joys and heartaches you have given them. They may be asking what it is they are supposed to learn from you. Your parents may be asking themselves if there is something special they should be doing for you. They also wonder what special reason brought you into their lives as opposed to another family's life. Adopting a child can ignite a desire for a deeper understanding of life. They are trying to figure out how all of you fit into the grand plan of life just as you may be doing.

Fear of Rejection and Abandonment. You may be surprised to learn that your parents fear you will reject them. They may feel rejection from you at certain times during your teen years. They may feel rejection over your friends, your interest in searching for your birth parents, your actual relationship with your birth parents and when you start to move out of the house.

One of the first times your parents may fear rejection from you will happen when you choose to be with your friends more than them. It might be as simple as you choosing to go to your friend's house instead of out to eat with them on Friday night. Even though you have turned them down many times in favor of your friends, it is different once you become a teenager. Your parents may have forgotten this is a normal part of growing up. Your parents may assume your decision to be with your peers over them is somehow the result of their parenting abilities. If your parents start telling you that you have been spending too much time with your friends, try suggesting a shared activity. This may even stop them from "nagging" at you so much.

If you are in a closed adoption, feelings of rejection may surface in your parents if you start asking questions about your birth parents. Your parents may feel they have failed raising you since you want to find your biological parents. If you share your plans from Chapter One with your parents, they will stop reacting emotionally and start helping you in your search. You can assure them, at least in most cases, that when adoptive parents share biological information with their adoptive children the relationship actually grows stronger (Kryder 1999).

Now if you are in an open adoption, your parents may interpret your separation as you wanting to live with your biological parents. Your parents may be feeling threatened by your birth parents, especially if you are able to connect with them on a different level. They may be afraid your birth parents will somehow convince you to live with them. Your parents may unintentionally make you feel you need to choose between them and your birth parents. If you feel this describes your parents, talking to them about the pressure you are dealing with will help get your life back to normal.

Many times rejection issues surface when you begin talking about going to college or starting a career which involves a move away from home. Regardless of the amount of love between you and your parents, they may wonder if you will forget about them. Once again, open communication with your parents is the best solution. Do not be afraid to ask your parents what they are thinking.

Loss. Just as you may feel the loss of your birth parents, your parents' feelings of loss can come from two different sources. Fertility issues can come into play once again. The other source of loss can occur when you leave home.

A lot of attention has been given to situations where adoptive parents have not resolved fertility issues while adopting a child. Counselors are studying what happens to adopted children who are raised in a family where fertility issues are still a problem. In fact, many adoption agencies require infertile couples to prove they have resolved all infertility issues before they are allowed to adopt a child.

If your parents did not come to grips with fertility problems before you were adopted, you may feel pressured by your parents to act a certain way. Does your mother relentlessly push you into piano lessons even though you despise going to them? Does your dad spend every weekend trying to improve your athletic skills even though you would rather be doing something entirely different?

Your parents, just like all parents, had a fantasy child in mind before they started trying to have children. They saw this fantasy child doing all sorts of activities, acting a certain way and even accomplishing certain goals. Under normal circumstances, your parents would have dealt with their inability to have children and accepted you as the unique person that you are right now. Instead, they believed adoption would cure their loss of this fantasy child. When you were adopted, you assumed the role of this fantasy child.

Let's assume your mother was the one who did not deal with this dream child. She probably found it difficult to provide the emotional support you needed while growing up. She expects you to behave like her fantasy child. This is not realistic and only results in adjustment problems for her and potentially you. You may feel unloved or unwanted by your mother.

However, keep in mind even parents without adopted children have a vision of a fantasy child that results in parental pressure to be a certain way. You probably have friends with parents like this. Can you think of a friend whose parents are avid golfers and insist that their child will be an avid golfer, too? Your friend plays in golf tournaments on the weekends, instead of developing his own interests, just to make his parents happy. This type of parent is fairly common, but sometimes just being adopted can create even stronger negative feelings toward your parents when they pressure you into doing things that you do not want to do.

Additionally, feelings of loss can develop during adolescence as they watch you mature and establish your own identity. They know eventually you will leave their home to live your own life. Just the idea of you leaving may trigger feelings of loss. If your mother has not developed outside interests while raising you, she might have difficulty adjusting to life after you move out of the house. Eventually she will adjust and things will get back to normal for her, but in the meantime you may feel she is not giving you enough space to grow. You can help by encouraging her to start a hobby, take a class or even work part-time.

Super-Parent Scrutiny. From the time your parents decided to adopt you, their lives have been scrutinized, analyzed, and picked apart by total strangers. Their destiny, and yours, was at the mercy of these strangers who searched for flaws in their personalities, abilities, intellect, and potential parenting skills.

The pressure did not stop when they finally adopted you. In fact, it may have become stronger. Now that you are finally their child, they may believe it is their mission as adoptive parents to make your life as happy and fulfilling as humanly possible. Additionally, some adoptive parents feel they need to prove not only to themselves but also to other family and friends they can be good parents. They question every decision they make. They wonder if they are too harsh or not harsh enough with every consequence they hand down to you.

If you are in an open-adoption family, your parents may feel the need to compete with your biological parents. The outcome will be super parents who invest a great deal of time making sure you have everything you need to be happy, especially if they fear you may leave them or your birth parents may take you away.

Fertility issues emerge again when parents feel they have to work harder at being good parents due to underlying fertility problems. If your parents failed at conceiving a biological child on their own, they may fear failing at parenting, too. In order to overcome their fears they become your super parents. The end result for your super parents is unnecessary stress.

Communicating with You. Some adoptive parents have difficulty talking about adoption with their children. If you live in a household in which adoption is rarely brought up, you are not alone. Many adoptive parents do not discuss adoption issues with their teenager. Your adoptive parents may react this way to protect you from telling you too much information. Also, your parents may feel uncomfortable thinking about the fact that you have another set of parents beside themselves, especially after they have devoted so much time trying to be the best parents possible.

Your adoptive parents might have difficulty deciding how much information to tell you. They may feel you are not emotionally mature enough to handle the information. They do not want to hurt your feelings or send you into an emotional crisis. Maybe they are waiting for that perfect moment that never arrives.

Once your parents begin talking about your adoption, your birth parents become concrete and real. The whole idea of this discussion brings out many worries for them. They do not know what your reaction is going to be if they bring up your adoption. They may fear trying to answer your questions, especially if they do not have any information or if the answers are not the ones they would like to give you. For instance, telling you that your birth mother abused drugs would definitely be difficult. They would rather avoid that discussion until absolutely necessary. Their ultimate fear is you will want to meet your birth parents and maybe even decide you want to live with them.

Also, your parents may think you do not want to talk about your adoption if you have not brought the topic to their attention. They might assume you do not think about it if you do not talk about it. Your parents are unlikely to start a conversation about something that does not appear to be a problem, especially if they do fear the conversation in the first place.

One thing to keep in mind when dealing with your parents is that they are people, too. They have feelings, many the same as you. It is not always easy being a parent. Many decisions have to be made. They scrutinize every decision they make in regards to you. That is a lot of pressure for your parents.

Now that you know why your parents have difficulty talking to you about your adoption, you can use this opportunity to show your maturity by opening the lines of communication yourself. Check out Chapter Six for tips on how to talk to your parents.

Chapter Three

Birth Mothers

Birth mothers will be the main focus of discussion in this chapter for two reasons. First, when adoptees think about their biological parents the birth mother immediately comes to mind. Second, adoptees that decide to search for their birth parents usually begin searching for their birth mother first. However, the story below does give some insight into how some birth fathers feel.

> *When I was contacted by my birth father about meeting, I informed him I wanted some answers to questions that I had been wondering about for years. He explained everything in great detail eventually. He answered all of my questions. Not only did I get my answers but I also learned how his life was affected. He clearly had a difficult time accepting he had a child somewhere in the world that he didn't get to see grow up. He later told me his entire outlook on life changed after we met.*

Each birth mother has unique experiences and feelings in making her decision to place her child for adoption. Birth mothers face pressures from society, her family, and herself in making the decision to place her child with another family. No two situations are alike except for their wishes to see their children grow up in a good home. The following description of a birth mother's experiences is not necessarily representative of all birth mothers, but the story contains elements that are common in many birth mothers' stories. Chances are your birth mother felt many of the same emotions.

Making the Decision. Your birth mother was probably young and not in a financial position to raise a child. From the day she found out she was pregnant with you her family pressured her into choosing adoption by telling her she couldn't possibly raise a child properly at such a young age. She may have also been emotionally and physically threatened by her own parents to choose adoption or abortion.

> *Every night when I would go to bed my mom would come in and say, "I know it's a hard thing to do and I don't feel especially good about it, but I just think it would be better if the baby had two parents and had a good life. Hopefully they will be parents with money and the baby can have whatever the baby needs and never have to do without." I thought that did sound good for the baby, but it just didn't feel right to me. I just listened to her. I never said okay or anything. Then she would leave the room and my dad would come in and say, "I know she just has the baby's best interest at heart, but we have money and that baby will not go without." Then he would go to bed and then I would be left there thinking about it.*

Your birth father was probably young and in the same position as your birth mother. Maybe he refused to provide any financial or emotional support. Maybe he was completely absent.

> *I was twenty years old. I had been in a relationship with this young man for about a year. We had talked seriously about getting married, but the romance was beginning to go downhill. Truly the romance had just run its course. Then I found out that I would be having a little one. I wanted the father to care and for us to paste the relationship back together, but he wanted no part of that.*

Your birth mother may have known from the beginning that placing you with another family was the only choice she had. Sometimes life's circumstances are such that no other decision could have been made other than adoption.

My dad committed suicide when I was a young teenager. My mom and I had never gotten over it. He did not leave a note explaining why and we were both devastated. I could not make a decision to keep my child and do that to my mother. We honestly were still so damaged by his death that we could not have done a good job with a baby. I wanted the best for my baby and he went to a place that I believed he would have the best chance at life. Also, my mom was a perfectionist and having been raised by her I could not give my baby a perfect home. Therefore, I should not keep the baby. At that time in my life I had no other understanding of how to proceed through life.

Even if your birth mother knew from the beginning that placing you with another family was the right thing to do, she had many undecided feelings throughout the whole pregnancy. In addition to the pressures from everyone around her, she most likely struggled daily during her pregnancy with the decision of what she was going to do about you. She changed her mind continually about whether adoption was the right choice.

I hope and pray my child hasn't been hurt by me.

After the Adoption. Your birth mother's life has been significantly altered by her experiences. She has never been able to return to her previous life as people promised she would be able to do. Immediately after you were adopted she struggled to move on with her daily routine. Her routine may have been studying in high school or college, working or just surviving.

Regardless of your birth mother's specific situation, she moved through a series of five stages to resolve her grief. Grief is a feeling that accompanies loss. Most people see grieving as a normal reaction to the death of a loved one. Our society has a more difficult time understanding that a mother who places her child for adoption will grieve for her child the same as someone whose child died.

The grieving process consists of denial, guilt, anger, sadness, and resolution. This process begins during pregnancy and continues until she moves through all of the stages. Birth mothers move through the stages at their own rate. Some do not make it through all five. Instead they get stuck in one stage without ever making it to the resolution stage.

Denial. When your birth mother found out she was pregnant with you she may have been so shocked that she reacted by denying she was even pregnant. She may have blocked her pregnancy out of her mind until she could no longer deny she was pregnant. She may have even denied the pregnancy until she went into labor with you. You may wonder how she could possibly be pregnant and not know she was pregnant, but it is possible that she really did not know she was pregnant.

> *I literally didn't think about being pregnant. I was in such denial. I ignored the whole thing. It never occurred to me I could be pregnant. I think I probably realized it when I started to noticeably gain weight in one spot and there is movement that goes along with it, but I never really told my mom. I don't know how I thought I would pull that off. I guess it was one of those daydreams where you just ignore it and it will resolve itself. At fifteen you would be in denial.*

Your birth mother may never have left the first stage of denial. If you do contact your birth mother she may not even acknowledge you are her child. She will not answer your phone calls or respond to your letters. She may even deny she had a child let alone placed one for adoption.

Guilt. Your birth mother then started to feel guilty about the position that she had gotten her into during such a difficult time. She felt guilty for letting her family down. She felt guilty for thinking about abortion and adoption. She felt guilty for "giving her child away."

If your birth mother does not work through this stage during pregnancy she may hide her past from other relationships. If your birth mother was in college she may have found reasons not to go home. By doing this she felt a sense of relief by not having to tell anyone she was pregnant. On the other hand, she felt guilty she could not even tell her own family about her situation.

The guilt may not have stopped at the pregnancy. Once she got married she may have kept the secret from her husband. Your birth mother feared revealing her secret out of fear she would lose her husband by telling him the truth. She may have felt so guilty she did not have any more children, because she felt she did not deserve another chance at raising a child.

Anger. Next she becomes angry with herself and the people around her. She is angry because she let herself get into a difficult situation. She is angry because her friends cannot relate to what she is going through at the moment. She is angry with her parents for pushing her into making tough decisions. She is angry because her boyfriend was not supportive. Maybe she is angry because he was too supportive and that made her adoption decision that much more difficult.

If your birth mother does not resolve her anger, she will proceed through life with a trail of broken relationships. Her relationships will be strained from the anger she directs at the people around her. This anger will keep her from developing healthy relationships with others in the future as well as in the present.

Sadness. After coming to terms with her anger, your birth mother felt sad she had to place you with another family. She probably spent a great deal of time crying over her loss. She had a difficult time dealing with all parts of her life after you were adopted. If she attended college or high school, she found it difficult, if not impossible, to study. If she worked, she struggled to keep her attention focused on her job.

If she did not deal with her feelings of sadness, she probably developed depression. Counseling and medication may have been necessary. If she experienced depression, her choices in relationships may have put her at risk for being taken advantage of or abused by others. This stage may affect her for the rest of her life.

Resolution. Once she worked through these previous stages, she finally accepted her life and the decisions she made. She is able to look back on her experiences and realize there was a greater good in the end for her child. Hopefully she was able to progress to this point.

> *Now that I'm older I don't regret what I went through if it brought another soul into life and brought happiness to a couple that could not have children otherwise.*

> *I feel that I truly did the best thing for the child, because I would not have been the kind of mom he needed at the time. I was still pretty unstable myself at that time and could not have raised a child in a good way, in a way that would have given him a proud self-esteem.*

Just because your birth mother has resolved her own adoption issues, this does not mean she has forgotten you. In fact, she probably thinks about you more often than you might imagine. Your birth mother may find your birthday unbearable. She may relive the pain of placing you for adoption every year on your birthday. She might go into a short depression that time of year. She may anticipate she will be sad on that day and so she will stay home from work. She may even spend the day completely alone.

On the other hand, she may react to your birthday in a different way. She might celebrate your birthday by creating rituals that are performed every year on that date. She might write letters to you with the intent of someday delivering them. She is definitely affected every year on your birthday.

Your birth mother may express sad feelings during other key times throughout her life. She becomes sad when she thinks about missing your first word and first steps. She might have become upset in August of your fifth year, because she did not get to take you to your first day of kindergarten. She thinks about you on holidays. She wishes deeply she could have attended your junior-high graduation.

> *I would like to know every detail of his life; how old was he when he started walking, what was his first word, what was his favorite food as a baby, did he cry or sleep through the night, was he an action kind of kid or did he like to read, who was his first girlfriend, could I please have pictures.*

Your birth mother probably looks at children about the same age as you and wonders if that teenager might be you. This is especially true if she lives in the same city where your adoptive parents live. She may spend a great deal of time noticing all the teenagers walking around her. Your birth mother clearly has not forgotten you.

In addition to working through her emotions, she most likely fantasizes about you just like you fantasize about her. Here is a list of common questions birth mothers wonder about their adopted children:

- Is she still alive?
- How is she performing in school?
- Does she receive good grades?
- What are her talents and interests?
- Is she planning on going to college?
- How are the adoptive parents treating her?
- Are they as wonderful as I imagined them?
- Do they treat her fairly?
- Does she have any siblings?
- Do they spend a lot of time doing family activities together?

Much research has been done on birth mothers' feelings toward placing a child with another family. The general consensus is birth mothers do want to raise the children they delivered at birth, but unfortunate circumstances made it impossible to keep their children. With this said, your birth mother gave you the best present ever and that is the gift of life. Your adoptive parents gave you the best life they could have given you through their support and commitment to your happiness.

> *I wished so much that there would have been some way that I could have known him, even if he did not know who I was, so that I would know how his life evolved. I really missed something there and I know it.*

Chapter Four

Searching

Just like all issues revolving around adoption, searching is no different. There is no right or wrong decision regarding whether to search. Some adoptees decide not to search. They do not have the inner drive to search out their birth parents. However, other adoptees have an intense urge to search. Others wish to search but do not out of fear of hurting their parents' feelings. If you are thinking about searching, several factors need to be considered before seeking out your birth parents.

Recent Changes to Help Searchers. Now that adoption has become much more acceptable and open in our society, adoptees are demanding information about their birth parents. No longer are adoptees afraid to raise questions and demand answers to those questions.

Likewise, biological parents who felt forced to place their child for adoption are taking steps to make contact with their child. Birth parents do not always have to wait until the child turns eighteen to start the search. Adoption agencies are more willing now to contact the adoptive parents to discuss reunions between the adoptee and their birth parents. Also, adoptive parents are becoming more agreeable in allowing their child to meet the birth parents to satisfy their curiosity and deal with emotional issues affecting their child.

In addition to changes in attitudes among the adoption triad, legal reforms and changes in adoption agency policies have made reuniting birth parents with adoptees easier than ever before. No longer are records sealed for life. Courts and social service workers are realizing the benefits of opening adoption records in some cases. Some states have completely opened their adoption records. Many others are establishing registries to assist birth parents and adopted children in reuniting with each other.

Deciding to Search. Deciding to search is much more complicated than calling the adoption agency and asking for your birth parents' information. Emotional maturity, your parents' willingness to help you, and your friends' support need to be looked at before you begin searching. All three of these factors are vital considerations as a teen searcher.

Emotional maturity is an essential ingredient in surviving the search process. A strong understanding of relationships will assist you in evaluating your situation at any given time during the search and reunion processes. Being able to understand that most relationships do not have clear-cut boundaries and are multidimensional will allow you to deal with all of the different emotions involved in meeting your birth parents.

> *I was a teenager when I met my birth mother. It was difficult for me to understand the dynamics of the relationships going on around me during those first few years. My birth mother clearly wanted to establish an ongoing relationship. I was more interested in writing letters occasionally. I didn't know how to stand up for myself. I was so overwhelmed by the whole situation that I stopped making contact soon afterward. It was a very traumatic time in my life. I should have waited until I was older to start searching.*

You can expect a roller-coaster ride of emotions while searching. You may be excited and fearful at the same time while anticipating a future contact with your biological relatives. One day you may be thrilled because you have a lead and then the next day be devastated because it did not work out.

Parental support is just as important as emotional maturity. Your parents need to be completely supportive of your decision to search. Your parents will be your emotional lifelines through the whole process. The stresses of searching combined with the daily trials of adolescence can be overwhelming at times. Also, your parents need to be able to be your advocate when you do finally meet your birth parents.

You will need your parents' financial assistance as well. Your parents will be the ones asking for the important information on your behalf. Sometimes this can be quite expensive. An attorney or private investigator may need to be hired. There will be potential trips to different cities or countries. Long-distance phone calls add up quickly, too.

Friends are an important part of your life. You probably spend more time with your friends right now than anyone else. Occasions will come up where you will break commitments with them. You may have to go out of town to collect information. Maybe you will have to cancel a date with your friends to catch up on missed schoolwork while you were gone. Having their support will help you in your search for your birth parents.

> **Have You Considered?!** What does your family really think about you searching for your birth parent? How committed are your parents in helping you search? How do you feel about sacrificing time from your friends to look for your birth parent? Are you able to step back from emotional situations to see the real issue or do you become an emotional train wreck?

Before the Search. Before you start the search process some very important decisions need to be made prior to starting your mission. You have to consider what you want the result to be in the end. Some people just want to know what their birth mother and birth father look like, if they have any siblings or just to let them know they have lived a good life with their parents. Often individuals begin searching in hopes of finding family medical and genetic information. Other searchers clearly want to meet their birth parents. On the other hand, some searchers want to express their anger at being placed for adoption or want to have tough questions answered. By defining your search goals, you will be better prepared for the actual contact.

I started asking my mom all of these different questions about my birth mother. I really just wanted some questions answered, wanted to see what she looked like and wanted to know if I had any brothers or sisters. Everybody else thought it would be no big deal. It just didn't work out that way. It was horrible. Things probably would have turned out better for me had I really thought about what I wanted to know before I started searching.

If you decide you want to meet your birth parents, you must decide how much contact is enough for you. You can always change your mind later. Many times one meeting is just enough to satisfy the curiosity. Others wish to establish a long-term relationship. The decision to meet your birth parents should not be taken lightly. That meeting will forever change your life, even if it is just once.

I would like to know everything from a distance. Just get the information really and then go to the next step.

Have You Considered?! What do you hope to accomplish in meeting your birth parent? What information do you need to start searching? Do you need hospital names? Do you need social service agencies? How will you get your birth parent's address and phone number? Do you need a private detective? Do you need an attorney? Can you do this on your own or do you have to have your parents' help? How much time and money are your parents willing to spend to help you locate your birth parent? How much time are you willing to spend searching? Do you have deadlines to help you meet your goals?

Transcontinental Searching. Searching in other countries may prove to be quite an experience for you. Some countries recently began to keep accurate birth records of children who have been adopted. Unfortunately, most adoptees that return to their native country to search for their birth parents do not obtain that information so easily.

Many times birth certificates have been lost, thrown out or never filed for transracial adoptees. Hospitals generally are not much help either since births oftentimes occur outside of the hospitals. Sometimes an orphanage worker will remember you as a small child. They may be able to give you some information to help you start on the right path. However, you must realize that finding your birth parents may be next to impossible.

If you wish to search for your birth parents in your native country, try checking out the options in that specific country. Just as in the United States, those birth parents are beginning to organize support groups to help them search for their child in the United States. You may get lucky.

> **Have You Considered?!** Have you checked out international adoption registries? Have you researched your home country's customs and traditions? Will you need an interpreter? How much money can you spend in travel costs? Where will you start searching once you get to the country? Who can help you search once you get there? Will the police help? Do you know the name of the orphanage where you came from? Do you have photos that can provide clues about your birth? What will you do if several women claim to be your birth mother? How do you think you will handle coming home without any information about your birth family?

During the Search. Once you start searching every aspect of your life will change. You must consider if this point in your life is the right time to start searching for your birth parents. Activities that you enjoy may become disrupted. Your friends may not be able to understand what you are going through. You may not be able to concentrate on the important things in your life once you start the search process. Events such as proms, homecomings, competitions, and striving for awards may become much less important to you.

For some the search process can become an obsession. Depending on your personality type, searching may become your number one priority over everything else. You may not be able to think about anything else except searching and all of the possible outcomes it will bring. Searching can take days, weeks or even years. If you are the type of person who sets goals and will not stop until they are met, you may want to consider scheduling a temporary break during your search.

Now that you know searching is not a simple process, you should also know that most people who have searched are satisfied with their decision to search. Even in the situations where the end result was disappointing, the searchers were glad they searched (Borders, Penny, and Portnoy 2000).

You may be wondering what will happen between you and your adoptive parents through the search process. You may be surprised to find your relationship has grown stronger. There are no more secrets or uneasy conversations taking place. Everything has been talked about at this point. This allows for a deeper relationship to develop between you and your parents.

> *My mom and I had a pretty open relationship. She always answered whatever questions she could for me. Through the whole search and reunion process I learned so much about my mom and her experiences that it really opened up a new kind of relationship between us.*

Have You Considered?! Have you planned to take a scheduled break from searching? Are your friends still supporting your decision to search? Are you missing important social events that you might regret later in life? What will you do if you cannot find your birth parent? When will you quit searching? What will you do if your birth parent contacts you first?

Chapter Five

Reunion

Now that you have the contact information, the first half of the battle is over and you can prepare for the second half. Now is the time to recharge and get yourself ready for that first contact with your birth parent. That is if you can wait!

Before Contact. Once you find your biological parent's contact information you will have to decide how you will contact her. Some people feel comfortable writing a letter while others want to make a phone call. Some people use their adoption agency as a mediator. Others think up more elaborate schemes such as pretending to be a Boy Scout selling popcorn or a telemarketer.

> *I used to imagine myself dressing up as a Girl Scout selling cookies. I pictured myself ringing the doorbell. I would sell some cookies to her and that would be it. I remained completely anonymous but still got to see what my birth mother looked like and where she lived.*

If you choose to write a letter or make a phone call, you will find books and Web sites to help you draft a letter or show you how to phrase that first phone call. While you are preparing your script, think about how much time you are willing to wait to try a second contact in case the first one is not successful. Think about what you will do if she hangs up on you if you choose to make a phone call. Sometimes birth parents do hang up because they are not prepared for the call. Deciding in advance if you will call back immediately, wait a while or write a letter instead can help you prepare for these unexpected responses.

Another real possibility in today's open adoptions is that you will be contacted first. Anticipating this event in advance will help lessen the shock if you are indeed contacted first.

> *I remember I answered the phone. There was a woman on the other end asking for my mom. This was not such an unusual thing to happen, but I remember knowing immediately it was her. It was such a shock to me. I couldn't eat, sleep or concentrate for many days after that phone call.*

Once a meeting has been arranged, an infinite number of outcomes are possible. Adoptees who have searched and made contact with their birth parents generally find themselves in one of five scenarios. There are others but these are the most common situations.

As you are reading the scenarios think back to the five stages of grieving for birth mothers. As you read the scenarios you will be able to tell which stage of the grieving process the birth mother is working through emotionally. Now that you understand the grieving process, you will see why there are so many different reunion outcomes.

Have You Considered?! How will you contact your birth parent once you have all of the information? Will you write a letter, make a phone call, write an e-mail or make a personal visit? What will you say when you first contact your birth parent? When you first meet will you shake hands, hug or wait until your birth parent makes the first move? Will you call your birth parent by their first name or by mom or dad? What will you say or feel if your birth parent does not want to talk to you? How fast do you want the relationship to move? Do you want a close relationship or one from a distance? Do you want to meet other biological relatives? If so, who would you like to meet?

Disappointed. If you have spent a great deal of time dreaming up what your birth parents may be like in real life, you may be disappointed to find out they are not what you expected. They may be poor, uneducated, living an abusive lifestyle or just plain mean. Perhaps they are perfectly nice but you just do not connect with them.

As mentioned before, it is not unusual for adopted teens to think of their birth parents as highly successful, wealthy or famous. In real life, not that many people fall into those categories. Chances are your birth parents fall somewhere in the average category. If you do have the opportunity to meet them, remind yourself they are likely going to turn out to be everyday people.

> *I had always dreamed she was wealthy and successful. Even though she ended up being a normal person I was a little let down to find out she wasn't as rich and powerful as I had imagined.*

Your birth mother might be a helpful secretary, a demanding office manager or someone who is abused by her husband. Your birth father could just as likely be an honest mechanic, rude store clerk or alcoholic. Being able to keep an open mind beforehand will minimize disappointments later.

If your birth parents fail to live up to even your minimum expectations, you do not have to have a relationship with them. You get to make the choices this time. If you can be honest with them about how you feel, do not worry about hurting their feelings. You will be hurting them even more by keeping in contact when you do not want to continue a relationship. You will be wasting your time and energy as well as theirs.

> *In those few years I had contact with my birth mother I was always trying to figure out ways to cancel visits. I didn't have the courage to tell my parents how I felt, so I ended having to continue to meet with her. The whole time she kept trying to build a relationship and I was miss-*

ing important weekends with my friends. It was not fair to either one of us.

Have You Considered?! How will you react if your birth parent does not live up to your expectations? Will you continue to give the relationship a try? Will you stop contact right then?

Turning Back Time. Let's assume you are meeting your birth mother, since this is the most common occurrence in adoption reunions. Birth mothers, as well as adoptees, sometimes feel the need to start over at the point of separation, usually birth. Your birth mother may still think of you as the infant she placed for adoption. She has not come to accept that you have grown up and lived a completely different life of your own. If your birth mother has not resolved her own feelings of guilt and loss of placing you for adoption, then she may want more from the relationship than you are willing to give. She may be emotionally demanding of your time and energy.

In this instance you can expect to feel more pressure to help your birth mother through this stage. This can leave you feeling drained by her neediness. She may wish to be more involved in your life than you would like. She may expect you to call her more, send more e-mails or write more letters. She may invite you to come to her house for extended stays. She may even want to come to your house more than you want her to come and visit.

If you find yourself retreating back to the time of separation, then you will need the extra attention from her. You will need to mentally work through your feelings of loss and separation you experienced while growing up. You may want her to make up for the affection she was not able to give you.

This is not to say these feelings are unhealthy. If you do experience these feelings and are given time to work through them, you will experience a tremendous sense of healing. These feelings can cross over into other parts of your life with benefits like improved relationships with friends and family. The same result can happen with your birth mother if she is given the chance to heal her wounds.

Even if you say today you will not feel this way, you still need to consider the possibility, because all rational thought will disappear at the time of reunion and shortly afterward. You cannot predict what you will feel when you finally meet your birth mother. Hidden feelings may come out of nowhere and need immediate attention.

The person who feels they need to travel back in time may desire to be touched more, hold hands often, give hugs and experience more tactile sensations in general. You need to prepare yourself for this possibility. If you do not feel comfortable at any time during your reunion, you need to make that known to your birth mother. This type of behavior can make you feel like you are being manipulated once again by someone in a situation in which you are not in control.

Always be frank about your desires and expectations with your birth parents and adoptive parents. You have to remember you are making the decisions this time. You are finally in charge of the direction of your life. Do not do anything you are not comfortable doing.

> **Have You Considered?!** How will you deal with a birth mother who wants more from the relationship than you? Are you strong enough to stand up for what you want? What will you do if you want more from the relationship than your birth mother wants to give? Will you wait or keep pushing?

More Secrets. Sometimes birth parents decide to keep their pregnancy and adoption a secret from their own family. This may seem like an impossibility, but such instances do occur. College women will conveniently stay at school for nine months without anyone thinking differently. Birth mothers may explain the weight gain as overeating. Maybe your birth mother decided to leave town to "try something new" until you were born.

This is especially easy for birth fathers since they are not the ones responsible for giving birth to the baby. Keeping a big secret, such as being an unwed father, is a relatively easy secret to keep from others. Nobody in the family, close or extended, can observe any visible signs of weight changes or temporary disappearances. This sort of scenario does not happen all that often, but under the right circumstances it could happen.

> *Right before I met my birth father and his family I was told that nobody in his family knew about me. I couldn't believe how he could keep such a big secret. The announcement to his family was just as much of a shock to them as it was to me.*

Your birth mother may have decided to keep you a secret, because she did not want to be pressured into changing her mind about placing you for adoption. Maybe she knew she was doing the right thing opting for adoption and she did not want other people trying to change her mind. If she was a career woman or in college, she may have kept this secret from her family out of fear her family would pressure her into raising you despite her desire not to have a family at that time.

If your birthmother does not want to divulge her secrets, then you have no choice but to continue with her secret. In this instance, a relationship will be very difficult to establish. You may develop feelings of resentment toward her for continuing to keep you a secret.

On the other hand, your birth mother, upon initial contact, may gladly tell her family about you and why she placed you for adoption many years previously. She will finally feel relieved to talk about her experiences after keeping you a secret for so long. You can expect a double shock from relatives that you not only exist but have been found, too.

Have You Considered?! Will your feelings be hurt if you have been kept a secret all these years? How will you feel if your birth parent wants to continue keeping you a secret? How long are you willing to be kept a secret?

You Can't Be My Child. This scenario is unlikely, but it is still a possibility. Your birth mother may not acknowledge she ever placed a child into adoption. She may have been so overwhelmed at the time of your birth that she completely blocked the event out of her mind. Placing you for adoption might have been such a trauma that she could not allow herself to think about the possibility that she has a child she did not raise on her own.

Another scenario is your birth father may not acknowledge you as a biological child either. Your birth mother may not have told him she was even pregnant with you. Maybe she did tell him she was pregnant with you and he didn't believe her or refused to believe her in order to protect himself.

On the positive side, even adoptees that have experienced this form of rejection report they are glad they searched. The end result may not have been what was expected, but these adoptees feel a sense of peace, resolution, and finality at the end of their search.

> **Have You Considered?!** How will you feel if your birth parent does not acknowledge you? Will you try to locate other relatives or quit searching altogether?

Unfortunate Circumstances. Some searchers find their biological parents incapacitated or unable to communicate with them. It is possible that your birth mother or birth father may be committed to a mental hospital, in prison or living in a nursing home or other type of rehabilitation center.

Your birth mother may have a debilitating mental illness in which communication is not possible. Perhaps an accident happened at some point in her life, which left her in a coma or with memory problems. She may have serious addictions that require constant care. Perhaps your birth mother has passed away.

In these instances you will have to make some serious decisions. If you cannot have a relationship with your birth mother, you may decide to seek out other biological relatives. If your birth mother is still alive but not able to communicate, a decision as to how much care you are willing to give her might be asked of you. In fact, family members may leave medical decisions up to you since you are next of kin. These are serious decisions for a teenager.

Have You Considered?! What will you do if your birth parent is ill? What will you do if you are asked to make life or death decisions about your birth parent? Will you try to find other birth relatives?

Other Reunion Issues. Other details have to be attended to as well outside of these scenarios. You and your biological family will have to agree on what titles will be used to address each other. How would you feel if a newly introduced biological aunt remarks, "You look just like your mom?" Will you take offense to someone calling your biological mother your mom? Some people may relish this thought while others may be offended.

> *I still feel resentful when someone from my birth mother's family refers to her as my mom even though we have since worked out our past differences. I'm not sure if I will ever get used to people referring to her as my mom.*

Another related topic is Mother's Day, Father's Day, and birthdays. You will have to decide if you want to recognize your birth parents on these particular occasions. Some birth parents may have their feelings hurt if you do not call or send cards to them on these special days. Other birth parents completely understand how you may be feeling and not pressure you into doing anything you do not feel comfortable doing.

> *I agonized over whether to send a Mother's Day card and birthday card to my mother that first year after we reunited. I decided to send a card for both occasions, but I tried to find ones that were generic. No one told me about these little details that can cause so much stress.*

Also, unexpected thoughts may creep into your mind after meeting your birth parents. You may be torn between which set of parents are your "real" parents. You may feel you need to choose between your adoptive and biological parents. You will have to expand your definition of parents to encompass your new family arrangements.

Teenagers sometimes fear their parents will let them live with their biological parents. Other times the fear is that the biological parents will take them away from the only parents they have ever known. Just remember, your parents are your legal parents. They have always been your parents. They will always be your parents. Your birth parents cannot take you away from them.

Another typical reaction is emotions tend to get carried away at the beginning of a reunion. A time-out can help you gain a clearer perspective on how you would like things to turn out in the long run. Do not hesitate to take a break to get used to your new family arrangements. Explain to your birth parents how you feel. Let them know you will tell them once you have made a decision about what step you want to take next. That next step could be forward or just staying where you are at the moment.

Also, you might share a common belief with other adoptees in which you believe once you meet your birth parents everything will be normal for you from an adoption standpoint, as if you are not adopted any longer. You will still be adopted. You will be an adoptee for the rest of your life. The feelings that come with being adopted will still be there after the reunion. Meeting your biological parents will not solve your problems. You will still be the same person with the same ambitions, dreams and difficulties.

Most importantly, you should always feel in control of the relationship. If you feel your relationship with your birth parents is moving too quickly or you just do not feel comfortable any longer with the arrangements, you have the right at any time to stop contact with your birth parents. You may find yourself wishing the reunion had taken place later in your life. Birth parents, as a rule, are just glad to have finally met you. Many birth parents report a willingness to give their child as much time and room as they need to sort out their feelings.

> *The reunion was a failure. I was too immature. If I had met my birth mother as an adult things would have turned out much better for both of us I'm sure.*

Have You Considered?! Have you discussed what titles you will use when you talk to each other? Where will you spend your holidays and birthdays? Will you go to extended family gatherings? Will you invite your birth parent to stay at your house? Will you stay at your birth parent's house? If so, for how long; a weekend, a week, a summer?

Tips for Successful Relationships. If you wish to improve your chances for a long-term relationship, you can easily make a few expectations clear before the relationship starts. You, your adoptive parents and your birth parents can start by agreeing on the direction of your relationships. You will need to establish realistic expectations for everybody involved in the reunion process by letting your birth parents and adoptive parents know whether you want to develop a long-term relationship or just want answers to your questions or something in between.

Agreeing on a time commitment from your birth mother is also important. If you do not have much time to commit, then your birth mother will not expect much. Maybe your birth mother has a life that does not allow for as many visits as you would like to have with her. By determining this in the beginning, you know what she can give. You will understand her circumstances when you have not talked to her in a while. Setting up a schedule for holidays, vacations, and birthday visits will help prevent hurt feelings for everybody when those times come up.

Establishing a preferred method of communication is also a good idea. If you are not comfortable with her calling you on the phone, let your birth mother know you would prefer to e-mail or write letters for now. This way your birth mother will know in advance not to give you personal phone calls. On the other hand, if you prefer phone calls, she will know not to e-mail or send you letters.

Also, many positive reunions begin with a flurry of letters, phone calls, e-mails, and visits. Eventually your eagerness to talk to each other will slow down. The letters, phone calls, and e-mails will not be so frequent. Do not be alarmed that your relationship is falling apart. The relationship is just moving to another level.

> *When my birth mother and I decided we wanted to really get to know one another, we were constantly talking, e-mailing, and planning visits with each other. I felt like I needed to make up for lost time. It was all just so exciting. I know I really put my whole family through a lot during that time period. After two or three months of this I finally got back into my old routine. Now we contact each other at our convenience. Something everyone can emotionally handle.*

Finally, taking anger and resentment into a reunion will hamper your efforts to build a relationship with your birth mother unless you are honest about your feelings from the beginning. If your anger is directed toward her, then allowing her to hear you talk about your feelings will be good for you, and probably her as well. If you do not tell her about your anger and resentment, then forming a solid relationship with her will be difficult.

> *Growing up I felt a lot of anger that my birth father just left my birth mother to make all of the decisions. I was resentful because I was denied the experience of growing up in a so-called normal family. My birth father and I had many problems establishing a relationship because I did not confront my birth parents with my feelings. Once I did that, I was able to move past my anger. We were able to form a somewhat normal relationship.*

Chapter Six

Talking to Parents

Adolescents are known for avoiding discussions with their parents. In fact, sometimes they avoid talking to their parents at all costs. However, teens have to talk to their parents about issues more serious than where they are going and when they will be home. For adoptees, the chance to discuss their adoption with their parents is something they would welcome.

Studies show 57 percent of adoptees would like to talk to their parents more about adoption. In one study two-thirds of adoptees reported having no discussion with their fathers about adoption during the previous year. Another 40 percent of adoptees stated no discussions with their mother had taken place either (Sheridan 2001). Clearly a communication gap about adoption is occurring between adoptees and their parents.

Many times adopted teens feel guilty asking parents questions about their adoption. If this describes yourself, you have a right to know the answers to whatever questions you may have. You should never feel guilty about wanting to know information regarding your birth parents. If you do not ask these questions, they will simmer and eventually boil over unexpectedly. Writing your questions down in a journal to ask at a later time can be helpful if you absolutely cannot talk to anybody.

Bringing up sensitive issues, such as adoption, can be particularly difficult for teenagers. If you find yourself nervous, just remember your parents are just as nervous as you. This will soon pass as you each begin talking about your ideas and feelings.

No protocols exist to tell you the perfect way to approach your parents. Each parent is different. Parents can be more approachable at different times of the day or on different days of the week. You will have to determine the best time to talk to your parents. Although, at this point in your life you probably have a pretty good idea when the best time is to approach your parents. Prepare your questions in advance so as to make them as clear as possible. Parents do not always add additional detail that is not asked.

Being open to all possibilities will allow you to accept the results of your conversation with your parents more easily. Most likely your parents will voluntarily give you whatever information they know, but be prepared for very little information or no information at all. Your parents may not have all of the information you are asking about or they feel giving you too much information will be harmful to you.

On the other hand, your parents may not be comfortable talking about your adoption at all. Do not become discouraged if your parents are not willing to talk about your adoption with you at that point. Maybe they need to think about what to say before they say it. You might have taken them by surprise. Give them some time to get used to the idea that you are starting to ask questions. You can always try later.

The following tips on how to approach parents have been offered by parents of teenagers themselves. As you read through the comments, think about how your parents have responded in the past when you have asked them for help with tough problems. This will help you decide how to approach your parents. Give it a try. Good luck!

When parents of adolescents are asked:
How would you like your teenager to bring up important issues with you?

> *I prefer straightforward honesty. My children should never be afraid to discuss any issue with me, whether they have done something wrong or just need an explanation.*

> *Straightforward, open, and honest.*

When he or she sees that it can be a quiet, undistracted time to talk.

To come right to me and ask.

Would you prefer to schedule a time to have an important discussion or have a discussion right at that time?

They can talk right at that moment but may be told to wait a moment until I'm not distracted.

Whenever my child feels like talking. A child should never have to schedule time to discuss important issues with his or her parents.

I trust my children to determine whether the issue is important enough to interrupt me. I don't want to schedule time. They are my children, not my employees. If they have to schedule time, they may not bother the next time.

Talk to me at the moment while it is on their mind instead of letting it get to them.

Under what circumstances would be the best time to bring up this issue?

When I'm not in the middle of something or when there is downtime.

During an activity that we are doing together would be ideal. Time of day is not a factor.

Ideally I think dinnertime is a great time to discuss important matters. Everyone is there and an open discussion with different opinions where different options can be discussed.

Dinnertime or in the morning.

Under what circumstances would be the worst time to bring up this issue?

During conflict or if I am in a hurry and cannot devote time to the issue.

If the parent is stressed over something else it probably wouldn't be a good time, but depending on the issue, it could be more important.

In front of other people who aren't involved could be avoided.

When cooking, working or when others are around.

What other suggestions would you offer teenagers who want to open up a discussion with their parents?

A positive attitude encourages a positive discussion.

Writing a note asking parents to take a few minutes to talk about something important.

Chapter Seven

Looking Forward

Like everything else about growing older, being adopted is a process that will continue throughout your life. You will acquire certain traits just by living your life as an adopted person. The traits will influence you throughout your whole life whether you like it or not. Fortunately, these traits give you big advantages over your nonadopted peers as an adult.

The first big payoff for you is that you have been raised under the ideal circumstances, at least for most of you. Researchers have shown that adoptive parents give their children more attention than nonadoptive parents give their children. Also, adoptive parents are generally successful, intelligent, and excellent role models. Additionally, adoptive parents provide their children with enriching opportunities that other children are not given, and adoptive parents provide exceptional support and encouragement in school and extracurricular activities. Finally, adoptive parents place a high value on family relationships (Fergusson, Lynskey, and Horwood 1995). If these statements describe your parents, you are indeed lucky to have them as your parents.

Second, the experiences of being adopted will help you to adapt to college, career choices, and increase your ability to appreciate differences (Kryder 1999). The stresses you encounter as a teenager will prepare you for the "real" world fairly well.

I've always had a good sense about relationships. People describe me as very independent. If I want something, I figure out how to get it. My life experiences, along with my natural talents, have certainly helped me get to the point I am today. I wouldn't change a thing.

Third, adoptees tend to develop strong commitments to their spouses, children, and extended family. Adoptees have a special appreciation for strong family ties. The following quotes are typical of adult adoptees.

> *Growing up I knew when I had kids I would be there for them whenever they needed me. I was determined to have a normal family. I have that and I appreciate every second of it. I've got my own family. We're not going to break this family unit.*

> *I always told myself that my kids would be my number one priority in my life. I promised myself to make a life for them that was normal. I believe I have accomplished that and they have a better life than had I not gone through all of the experiences I did as a child.*

> *I'm very needy. I want my hugs and kisses. I need a lot of love and attention, but through all of this I think I'm a terrific mom.*

Fourth, adoptees frequently become very committed to the careers they chose because of their adoption experiences. These careers usually focus on helping others in some way. In my case, I chose to go to college to study psychology and then special education in order to work with teenagers who experience difficulties in school or at home. A friend of mine went to college first to study legal processes so she could work toward helping adoptees have access to their adoption files. In fact, she worked with her state representatives to change the adoption laws in her state. She also strongly believes everyone has a right to their medical records. She has since gone on to get a degree in nursing that reflects her commitment to providing medical information to her patients. Many dedicated social workers and genetic researchers are also adoptees based on their experiences of growing up adopted.

Fifth, adoptees may find they have a deep religious or spiritual conviction. They start questioning why things happen and then try to make sense out of their world at an early age, much earlier than most people. They develop an attitude that life somehow has meaning even if it seems completely chaotic and uncontrollable. These beliefs help them weather the rough times in life easier than nonadoptees.

> *I feel that I ended up with my family, because God planned it that way. He is in control of all things. I was meant to be with my family. I was meant to live where I live. I was meant to marry who I married and have my children. Those things may not have happened if I had not been placed for adoption.*

As you can see, growing up adopted has some real advantages. Even though it seems this time in your life will last an eternity, it will pass before you know it. Once you become an adult, in just a few short years, you can start taking total control of your own life. But for now, remember the experiences you are going through will have long-lasting benefits when you become an adult. You are an adult much longer than you are a teenager, so you will have a lot of time to enjoy the benefits of the stress you are going through right now.

Additional Resources

Books

Where Are My Birth Parents?: A Guide for Teenage Adoptees by K. Gravelle and S. Fisher. Published by Walker and Company.

Searching for a Piece of My Soul by T. L. Kling. Published by McGraw-Hill.

How It Feels to Be Adopted by J. Krementz. Published by Alfred A. Knopf, Inc.

The Lost Daughters of China by Karin Evans. Published by Jeremy P. Tarcher/Putnam.

Teen Girls Only: Daily Thoughts for Teenage Girls by Patricia Hoolihan. Published by Holy Cow! Press.

Bibliography

Affleck, Marian K., Lyndall G. Steed. 2001. "Expectations and Experiences of Participants in Ongoing Adoption Reunion Relationships: A Qualitative Study." *American Journal of Orthopsychiatry* 71:38–48.

Benson, Peter L., Anu R. Sharma, and Eugene C. Roehlkepartain. *Growing Up Adopted: A Portrait of Adolescents and Their Families.* Minneapolis: Search Institute, 1994.

————. "New Study Identifies Strengths of Adoptive Families." Search Institute Archives (1997), from http://www.search-institute.org/archives/gua.htm (accessed March 8, 2003).

Blomquist, Barbara T. *Insight into Adoption: What Adoptive Parents Need to Know about the Fundamental Differences between a Biological and an Adopted Cchild—and Its Effect on Parenting.* Springfield, IL: Charles C. Thomas Publisher, LTD, 2001.

Borders, L. DiAnne, Judith M. Penny, and Francie Portnoy. 2000. "Adult Adoptees and Their Friends: Current Functioning and Psychological Well-being." *Family Relations* 49:407–418.

Christian, Cinda L., Ruth G. McRoy, Harold D. Grotevant, and Chalandra M. Bryant. 1997. "Grief Resolution of Birth Mothers in Confidential, Time-limited Mediated, Ongoing Mediated and Fully Disclosed Adoptions." *Adoption Quarterly* 1:35–58.

Cohen, Shari. *Coping with Being Adopted.* New York: The Rosen Publishing Group, Inc., 1988.

Cubito, David S., and Karen O. Brandon. 2000. "Psychological Adjustment in Adult Adoptees: Assessment of Distress, Depression, and Anger." *American Journal of Orthopsychiatry* 70:408–413.

DuPrau, Jeanne. *Adoption: The Facts, Feelings, and Issues of a Double Heritage.* Englewood Cliffs, NJ: Julian Messner, 1990.

Evans, Karub. *The Lost Daughters of China: Their Journey to America, and a Search for a Missing Past.* New York: Jeremy P. Tarcher/Putnam, 2000.

Fergusson, David M., Michael Lynskey, and L. John Horwood. 1995. "The Adolescent Outcomes of Adoption: A 16-Year Longitudinal Study." *Journal of Child Psychology and Psychiatry* 36:597–615.

Frankel, F. *Good Friends Are Hard to Find.* Los Angeles: Perspective Publishing, 1996.

Gladstone, James, and Anne Westhues. 1998. "Adoption Reunions: A New Side to Intergenerational FamilyRelationships." *Family Relations* 47:177–184.

Goodwach, Raie. 2001. "Does Reunion Cure Adoption?" *Australian/New Zealand Journal of Family Therapy* 22:73–79.

Gravelle, Karen, and Susan Fischer. *Where Are My Birth Parents?: A Guide for Teenage Adoptees.* New York: Walker and Company, 1993.

Grotevant, Harold D. 1997. "Family Processes, Identity Development, and Behavioral Outcomes for Adopted Adolescents." *Journal of Adolescent Research* 12:139–161.

Grotevant, Harold D., Nicole M. Ross, Mary Ann Marchel, and Ruth G. McRoy. 1999. "Adaptive Behavior in Adopted Children: Predictors from Early Risk, Collaboration in Relationships within the Adoptive Kinship Network, and Openness Arrangements." *Journal of Adolescent Research* 14:231–247.

Kinn, Gail. *Be My Baby: Parents and Children Talk about Adoption.* New York: Artisan, 2000.

Kling, Tammy L. *Searching for a Piece of My Soul.* Berkley, CA: McGraw-Hill, 1997.

Krementz, Jill. *How It Feels to be Adopted.* New York:Alfred A. Knopf, Inc., 1982.

Kyrder, Sandra. 1999. "Self and Alma Mater: A Study of Adopted College Students." *Child and Adolescent Social Work Journal* 16:355–372.

Lenkowsky, Linda K. 1998. "The Behavioral and Psychological Adjustment, Family Functioning, and Adoption Dynamics of Adopted Adolescents Growing Up in Biological-Adoptive Families, Compared with Adopted Adolescents Growing Up in All-adoptive Families." *Dissertation Abstracts International* Section B: Sciences & Engineering, 59 (7-B):3736.

Lifton, Jean. 1999. "The Adoptee's Journey." *Journal of Social Distress and the Humanities* 11:207–213.

Martin, Allison. "Resolving the Loss of Fertility" (2000), from http://www.comeunity.com/adoption/infertility/infertility.html (accessed March 22, 2003).

Maughan, Barbara, Stephan Collishaw, and Andrew Pickles. 1998. "School Achievement and Adult Qualifications among Adoptees: A Longitudinal Study." *The Journal of Child Psychology and Psychiatry* 39:669–685.

McRoy, Ruth. "Changing Adoption Agency Practices: Mental Health Implications for Birth Parents, Adoptive Parents, and Adopted Children." Center for Social Work Research, University of Texas at Austin, from http://www.utexas.edu/research/cswr/projects/pj0127.html (accessed February 11, 2003).

Miller, Brent C., Fan Xitao, and Harold D. Grotevant. 2000. "Adopted Adolescents' Overrepresentation in Mental Health Counseling: Adoptees' Problems or Parents' Lower Threshold for Referral." *Journal of the American Academy of Child and Adolescent Psychiatry* 39:1504–1511.

Powledge, Fred. *So You're Adopted*. New York: Charles Scribner's Sons, 1982.

Rosenzweig-Smith, Janet. 1998. "Factors Associated with Successful Reunions of Adult Adoptees and Biological Parents." *Child Welfare League of America* LXVII: 411–422.

Sheridan, Tim. "Relatedness Deprivation: A Review of the Search Institute Study of Adopted Adolescents and Non Adopted Siblings." Search Institute (2001), from www.netaxs.com/~sparky/adoption/sir.htm (accessed on February 24, 2003).

Silverstein, Deborah H., and Sharon Kaplan. "Seven Core Issues in Adoption." From www.adopting.org/silveroze/html/lifelong_issues_in_adoption.html (accessed February 24, 2003).

van den Akker, O.B.A. 2001. "Adoption in the Age of Reproductive Technology." *Journal of Reproductive and Infant Psychology* 19:147–159.

Wadia-Ells, Susan. *The Adoption Reader: Birth Mothers, Adoptive Mothers, and Adopted Daughters Tell Their Stories*. New York: Avalon Publishing Group, 1995.

Reader's Guide

Overview

Congratulations! You are the first group of teenagers to go through adolescence with knowledge of your birth history and access to your birth records. Some of you have limited information, some of you have a lot of information, and the rest of you fall somewhere in between these two extremes. Adult adoptees, on the other hand, have to fight for information about their birth parents. Oftentimes they find very little or no information at all. Their birth records have been sealed and locked away forever. Your generation is asking questions and getting answers. This recent change in adoption practices has created some interesting and unpredictable challenges for adoptees, birth parents, and adoptive parents. *Adopted Teens Only: A Survival Guide to Adolescence* is a tool to help you sort through and organize your thoughts and feelings about being adopted.

After reading this book, you may have decided you want to learn more about the experiences of other teen adoptees. The purpose of this reader's guide is to provide you with a valuable and practical tool to guide discussions between you and other adopted teenagers. Meeting others and talking about your own story can help you deal with the challenges that come with being adopted. Likewise, your story can help others deal with their own challenges of being adopted. You may even make some new lifelong friends along the way.

The discussion questions are meant to be conversation starters for groups of teen adoptees. You'll soon find that there are other teens who have had the same experiences as you. You may have had the same fantasies, felt the same anger, and had the same struggles with your parents. Of course, you will meet a lot of other adoptees who have led completely different lives.

Since you are a teenager growing up in a digital world, the possibilities of connecting with other adopted teenagers are nearly endless for you. If you would like to visit a monitored and safe site, please check out www.daneagorbett.com to hear what other adopted teenagers have to say. You can even post your own comments if you would like. (And of course, don't forget to ask your parents first.)

Interview with Danea Gorbett

1. What inspired you to write *Adopted Teens Only?*

As a teenager, I had a very close friend who was adopted and knew nothing about her biological family, and I had friends who knew their fathers but not their mothers. Then there was myself. I knew my mother but not my father. Regardless of our different situations, we still fantasized about our unknown biological parent(s); we wanted to know more about them and felt different levels of anger, loss, and abandonment. We had to deal with issues related to searching, and some of us had to make difficult decisions once we found our biological parent. My experiences, and my friends' experiences, are fairly similar to what adopted teenagers are going through today in open and semiopen adoptions. I felt by writing *Adopted Teens Only,* I could help prepare teen adoptees for some of the difficulties and decisions they are likely to face in the upcoming years.

2. How did you decide on the topics to focus on in the book?

As I was developing the content for this book, I looked at my own experiences and the experiences of other adoptees. Some of these adoptees were friends, friends of friends, relatives of friends, and teenagers that I worked with over the years in education and through adoption networks. Once I organized what I wanted to write about, I then reviewed research studies, surveys, and case studies to make sure what I was writing about was indeed common to adoptees, especially teenagers.

3. Adopted teenagers are often curious about the experiences of others who have searched for or been contacted by a

biological parent in their teenage years. You said in the introduction that you met your biological father for the first time when you were a teenager. Do you recall what you were thinking and feeling during the days you were waiting to meet your biological father and the rest of the family?

I tried very hard to keep focused on school and friends. Despite my best efforts, I was an emotional wreck during those few days. I knew the time had come to see if my biological father was the father I had always imagined, a wealthy and wildly successful person who lived in a mansion and couldn't wait to include me in his extravagant lifestyle of traveling and shopping. I also thought about all of the questions that I wanted to ask about the time when my mom was pregnant, my birth, and the years afterwards. I wanted to know why he made the decisions he made back then. I thought about what to wear, what I was going to say when we would be introduced, whether to hug or shake hands, and whether to say "Nice to meet you" or "Where have you been all my life?" Needless to say, it was very difficult to sleep, to eat, or to concentrate on anything other than what was about to take place in my life.

4. What was that first meeting like with your biological father?

At first it was terrifying. The only family I had ever known allowed me to go with a complete stranger to another city sixty miles away to meet a father I had never known. I was surprised to find out that my biological father was not wealthy but just a normal person with a normal job and a normal house. I also found out that I had a stepmom and very young brothers. For the most part, the day consisted of making small talk about school, sports, and hobbies. I even got a lot of my questions answered, except the ones about my birth. By the end of the day, I was definitely ready to go home and get back to my normal life. However, my teenage years would never be normal again after that meeting.

5. What were some of your struggles as a teenager after you met your biological father?

I was forced to deal with the really tough issues of anger, abandonment, and loss. No longer could these feelings be ignored. I also felt a lot of pressure to make this relationship work out with this other family that I barely knew. Just at the time when I was really enjoying some freedom at home and at school, I felt forced to give up frequent weekends to build a relationship with my biological father and his family. What I really wanted was to go back to my "old" life and be able to spend the weekends with my friends and the family I had always known. Unfortunately, I was too young to deal with these complicated issues, even at the ripe age of fourteen. Nor did I know how to tell my mom that I no longer wanted to visit my biological father's family.

6. How have these experiences affected your life?

As a teenager, I constantly asked myself why I had to go through this and why I couldn't have a normal life like everyone else. By thinking about such complex issues at a young age, I actually learned how to analyze complicated life problems and most importantly how to understand life from multiple points of view. I also developed a sophisticated understanding of relationships that continues today. Additionally, my own experiences as a teenager help me sympathize with my high school students and their struggles with their parents and the different family lifestyles that exist in our culture. I also know that life for teens can be complicated, even when they pretend it's not.

7. What do you want readers to take away from *Adopted Teens Only*?

The most important thing for adopted teenagers to realize is that what they're feeling and thinking is completely normal. I also want the readers to be prepared for the challenges that come with being an adopted teenager. Whenever teenagers have to make decisions, they should be given as much information as possible so they can make positive choices. The decisions they make can affect their lives in many ways and for years to come. Hopefully this book will help guide the decision-making progress.

Topics for Discussion

1. There's a saying that adversity builds character, and adopted teenagers certainly have difficult issues to resolve during adolescence. In what ways has being adopted made you a stronger person? In what ways have you struggled with being adopted?

2. Research suggests that birth parents struggle greatly with the decision to find adoptive parents to raise their child. What factors should birth parents take into consideration before deciding to find adoptive parents for their unborn child? Are there circumstances where an unborn child should always be placed with an adoptive family?

3. Often teenagers want to know more information about their birth parents than their adoptive parents are willing to tell them. What types of information should adoptive parents share with their teenager regarding the adoption process? Are there circumstances or situations that should not be shared with their teenager?

4. If you are thinking about or are searching for a birth parent, what do you hope to find at the end of the search? Why are you searching?

5. Adoptees searching for birth parent records frequently find they have limited access to their own files. This can be very frustrating for the person searching. What types of information do you think adoptees should have a legal right to know? What types of information should birth parents be allowed to keep private?

6. How do the adoptees' quotes in the book compare to your own experiences? What stories could you add?

7. Some adoptive parents find talking about the adoption experience with their teenager difficult. Why do you think these parents struggle to talk about the adoption? What can teenagers do to help their parents talk openly and honestly about the adoption?

8. Sometimes, for various reasons, adoptive parents refuse to help their teenager search for a biological parent. Other times, adoptees do not want their parents to know they are searching for a biological parent. When is it acceptable for a teenager to secretly search for a birth parent? What obstacles do you think these teenagers might encounter while searching? What are the long-term consequences of secretly searching?

About the Author

Danea Gorbett grew up in a small town in Indiana. She was raised by her mother and adopted father. She met her biological father for the first time when she was a teenager. Her experiences inspired her to study psychology at Purdue University. Danea graduated from Purdue in 1990 with a bachelor of arts degree. After college, she worked with teenagers in foster care and group homes. Danea also has a master of science degree in special education from Northern Illinois University. Currently she teaches students with physical disabilities, learning disabilities, and emotional disorders in a large suburban high school outside of Chicago. Danea is actively involved in her community, serving on various committees that educate and support teenagers in making positive life choices. She lives with her husband, Rich, and two children, Richard and Abby, in Geneva, Illinois. In her free time, Danea enjoys the outdoors, especially horseback riding and volunteering at a horse rescue shelter.

978-1-58348-481-4
1-58348-481-7

LaVergne, TN USA
03 March 2010

174853LV00001B/109/A

9 781583 484814